W9-CBA-444

THE CLASH BETWEEN

CHRISTIANITY AND

CULTURES

THE CLASH BETWEEN
CHRISTIANITY AND
CULTURES

Donald McGavran

CANON PRESS
1014 WASHINGTON BUILDING
WASHINGTON, D.C.

ISBN # 0913686 12 3
Copyright © 1974 by Canon Press
1014 Washington Building
Washington, D.C.
Printed in the United States of America

Dedicated to
Mary Howard McGavran
my wife, without whose constant help
and encouragement this and other
books could not have been written

CONTENTS

CHAPTER ONE

MANY WAYS VERSUS THE ONE WAY

A mighty clash of convictions resounds around the world and will continue to reverberate during the coming decades. Men are deciding a most difficult question: *Is there One Way or are there Many Ways?* Hosts line up on one side and on the other. Cannons are wheeled into position and salvos fired. Lectures are delivered, courses are taught, and books are written on each side. The question begins with concrete customs and readily describable value systems, but it soon takes us into the realm of the Ultimate, where answers will be given in accordance with faith rather than sight.

These chapters discuss the question on the basis of three assumptions: first, that the cultures of mankind are rich beyond description, wonderfully adapted to the multifarious conditions under which men live, and have much to contribute to global progress and happiness; second, that Christianity as it spreads must fit each culture, adopt new customs, and adapt itself to diverse contexts; third, that God has made men of one blood and that at the level of redeemed humanity his will for men has been and is being authoritatively revealed in his Word.

I hope this book will help Christians see the issues involved in the contextual nature of Christianity and work their way through to decisions in harmony with biblical convictions.

1

I *The Many Ways*

It is increasingly clear that the world in which we live is multi-cultural. Men have not one pattern of life but many. Our 'global village' is not a village at all, but a huge metropolitan mosaic made up of tens of thousands of different cultural units. Society is a bewildering patchwork quilt of races, peoples, classes, and languages. Even in the extremely homogeneous population of the United States, the Republicans in the election of 1972 wooed more than fifty ethnic minorities. Christians in the city of Bombay alone worship in seventeen different languages. In short, myriads of rich cultures live side by side.

It is axiomatic in contemporary thinking that each culture has a right to live its own life. With the defeat of Hitler and his theory of the master race, the world swung enthusiastically to the doctrine that cultures were equal — one was as good as another. All were valid ways of life for those who practiced them. Cultural relativism has become a dogma in much modern thinking. Each culture has an inalienable dignity and right to exist; no man has a right to change it. Vast permissiveness marks current thinking. If a way of acting feels good to a given society or culture, it is *right* for it.

As men began to study the multitudinous cultures of mankind, they were first inclined to believe that cultures had evolved from simple, primitive forms to the complex and civilized; but then it became apparent that most students of culture were members of the civilized culture! It was easy to argue that their judgments (our own culture is advanced, mature, and civilized — in short, higher) were biased. Furthermore, primitive cultures were found to be complex and their people by and large satisfied with their style of life. It is also indubitable that if one despises a culture his study of it is not apt to yield real understanding. All of this helped produce the dogma that no one way is right. There is no absolute right and no universal morality. On the contrary, all that really exists is a multitude of cultural standards and patterns each of which is right for its adherents.

With the formation of the League of Nations and later the United Nations, scores of new nations from Africa, Asia, and other sections of the world aggressively defended the thesis: "Our culture is as good as any." Magazines such as *National Geographic* flourished, edited according to the dogma of cultural relativism. They never speak ill of any culture nor point out its weaknesses. Unfavorable evidence is suppressed or explained away. Cultural relativism rules the press.

Add to these causative factors the guilt complex of postwar Europe and America. So much of the conflict and injustice in the modern world has been caused by powerful western nations seeking to impose their rule, trade, values, and ideologies on one another and on underdeveloped nations. Curiously, at the very time that thousands of the ablest men of developing nations flock to Europe and America for study, employment, and citizenship, leading voices of the West proclaim its culture decadent and not as good as that of the Iroquois or the Montagnards of Vietnam!

After two world wars and the rise of independent nations by the score, leaders in Europe and America, acutely conscious of western sins, call for penitence rather than claim maturity or advanced status for western culture. To be sure, their guilt complex does not square with reality. The Third World is avidly copying the western world in education, health, manufacture, national development, military equipment, and the whole bag of secular civilization at the very time that the guilt-smitten West is weeping copious tears at the memory of its unworthiness. The Third World would copy western political systems too —if it could operate them. But since these require a high degree of maturity, most emerging nations have shifted over to military dictatorships. In the West cultural and ethical relativism has free rein.

The tremendous vogue of agnostic philosophies (Marxism, scientism, positivism, and secularism) contributes significantly to the mood of cultural relativism. All these varieties of humanism maintain stoutly that man is on his own. Either there is no God, or he is securely chained by his creation. All religions are man-made. They are man's concepts of the universe, the Ultimate, the Absolute. They are in no sense revelation. Any idea of God disclosing himself (especially in a little known culture on the eastern shores of the Mediterranean Sea) is utterly unbelievable. It follows that if all religions — Christianity included — are simply what groups of men have thought, if the value systems of various cultures have been deified as a good way of enforcing them, then each has some good ideas and some bad ones, each has some truth and some error. Each is good for those who believe it, but claiming universal validity for it is going too far. The basic concepts of the religions are therefore equally true and equally false. All this makes an excellent philosophical base for cultural and ethical relativism.

As I am preparing these chapters, the January 13th *Star News* of Pasadena is carrying a feature story by G. W. Cornell headlined INDIAN RELIGION GAINS CHURCH RESPECT. The article develops the theme that American Indian religion may exceed Christianity both in its tolerance and communal character. The writer quotes Dr. Benjamin Reist, dean of the Presbyterian Theological Seminary at San Anselmo, as saying that Christian theology is "terribly impoverished when it comes to a doctrine of nature. There must come a day quite soon when American Indian theology must be represented in the highest councils of Christian theology in the world."

Most modern nations are congeries of different cultures which have to get along with one another. Adherents of each have to be guaranteed religious liberty, i.e., freedom to believe as they wish, freedom to worship Baal or Jehovah, Christ or Krishna, Allah or Buddha as they and their kinsmen desire. Since the state guarantees freedom of religion, it is an attractive—though strictly illogical — step to conclude that all religions must be equally true.

On the one side of the huge clash between Christianity and cultures stands cultural relativism stoutly maintaining that there are many ways to God, many good cultures, and many standards of right and wrong. Any attempt to persuade men of other cultures to your way of thinking is cultural imperialism. To cultural relativism, Christian missions are impertinent invasions of ethnic units whose members are happy and satisfied in their own customs and beliefs. These they have practiced from of old. Men have grown up in these cultures and feel at home in them. Missionaries should not trouble them. If men care to become Christians, they should bring their own customs with them. What business has Christianity trying to impose its own ethic and life style upon them? In short, cultures have the right of way.

Rajagopalacharia, the first Indian Governor General of India and a very great man, replied to Blaise Levai's question about missionaries as follows:

> It is not possible on the grounds of revelation, or logic, or on the evidence of miracles to hold that among the religions known as Hinduism, Jainism, Buddhism, Islam and Christianity any one is nearer to the truth than any other. I object to the exclusive claim for truth, if any, made on behalf of any one of these faiths . . . it is not desirable to make efforts for proselytization among them. Such efforts undermine their present faith, which is good enough for promoting right conduct and deterring them from sin, and tend to disturb family and social harmony.[1]

His opinion would be echoed by tens of thousands of Americans and Europeans.

All these factors I have described produce a climate of thought favorable to the conviction that when men of each culture live according to its patterns and precepts, they are living right. Pluralistic society inclines to cultural and religious relativism as water runs down hill. The belief in Many Ways seems reasonable to most men today.

II   *The One Way*

The second of the opposing forces is the Christian conviction that God has revealed to men the *one right way*. This way is clearly delineated in the Bible and in Jesus Christ and can be modified only by the action of the Triune God himself revealing new truth. The clash therefore is between the awesome array of men and nations which believe in many ways, many life styles, many cultures, each equally valid for its adherents, and Christians, who believe that God has shown men the true and living way and wants all men to walk in it.

Christians maintain, of course, that God has given a general revelation to all men. The Bible speaks of it again and again, perhaps most clearly in the first chapter of Paul's epistle to the Romans. He says: "What can be known about God is plain to them, because God has shown it to them. Ever since the creation of the world his invisible nature, namely, his eternal power and deity, has been clearly perceived in the things that have been made" (Rom. 1:19, 20). But this revelation, the Bible is careful to state, is precisely of God's invisible nature, his power and deity. The revelation is precisely *not* in human speculations as to sin and salvation nor in the idols and religious systems which support them. All these the Bible calls 'futile thinking'. In Acts 17:30 we read that, standing in the Areopagus in Athens, Paul declared that the whole polytheistic system was devised "in the times of ignorance" during which God for long years overlooked the sin and folly of idolatry, but now since the coming of Jesus Christ "commands all men everywhere to repent" and believe on Christ.

Aside from God's general revelation, which men have so rejected, and aside from conscience (an innate knowledge of right and wrong), which men have steadily violated, we have no sure knowledge about God outside of God's special revelation in the Bible and in Jesus Christ.

Christians agree that there are, indeed, many religions in the world with many teachings and practices which have much good in them. Good teachings and practices are clearly either men's discoveries or heavily colored light coming from God. Let us for a moment think of them as *men's discoveries*. Man is the great discoverer. He is constantly seeking to find out more about the universe. He has discovered mathematics, physics, chemistry, and other sciences. By the painful and laborious process of making and testing hypotheses, he has built up a reasonably accurate understanding of the physical universe. When in the next few years Mariner visits Mars and later Jupiter and Saturn, we shall discover still more. So we should expect considerable truth in the various religions and ethical systems men have worked out. But, since man is finite and is constantly revising his science as he learns more, the discoveries of the religions are never final truth. Christians hold that this comes only through Jesus Christ, who said:

> He who comes from above is above all; . . .
> He bears witness to what he has seen and heard . . . .
> He whom God has sent utters the words of God . . . ;
> the Father loves the Son and has given all things into his hand.
> He who believes in the Son has eternal life; he who
> does not obey the Son shall not see life. (Jn 3:31-36)

Let us now for a moment think of the teachings and practices of the world's religions as *colored light* coming from God. Let us assume that God *has* been speaking to the myriad writers of the non-Christian philosophies and scriptures. Then we must say that the divine light which streams through these teachings is heavily colored by man's guesses and sins. The teachings con-

tradict themselves. Some are high and noble, others low and
sordid. Some ring true, others are trivial, false, and grotesque.

Whether we regard religious teachings and doctrines as discoveries made by men or as colored light coming from God,
Christians rejoice in whatever truth is in them, but measure
it by the white light of God's revelation in Christ—the final
authority.

The Christian belief rests on the remarkable unity of revelation in the Bible. Though the books were written over a period
of a thousand years by men in every conceivable circumstance,
the teachings about God and man are consistent and unified.
This can be explained only by assuming the true and living God
did what the Bible asserts he did; namely, set forth the one way
of salvation, the one path for men to walk in, the one pattern
of righteousness which is pleasing to the Eternal God, the one
Church, the one faith, the one baptism, the one sure knowledge
about God. If told it is incredible that so great a truth could be
revealed to so small a nation and so undistinguished a culture,
Christians agree that it is incredible, but affirm it is what God
did. (I Cor. 1:27-28) Why it pleased him to reveal himself to
the Hebrew tribes and in the Son of a peasant girl is part of the
mystery. That he did so no Christian doubts. The entire Bible
proceeds on the assumption that God the Father Almighty,
Maker of Heaven and Earth, deliberately chose to make the
definitive revelation of himself in this way. And since the Bible
is the definitive revelation, all other ways may now — though
somewhat roughly—be judged by it. In the end, all other ways
— and empirical Christianity too — will be judged by Jesus
Christ according to how their adherents have received it.

A corollary of the one way (the one revelation, the one book,
the one Saviour, the one baptism) is that there is one Christian
culture. One way of acting, thinking, forgiving, worshipping,
repenting, and believing is pleasing to God. As this life style
takes shape in deeds, thoughts, institutions, buildings, customs,

languages, and dreams, the Christian culture is formed.

To be sure, the Christian culture has not been fully formed anywhere; rather, it is being approximated in thousands of cultures all over the world. In a few places, small whole societies have become Christian and devote their entire being to obeying the biblical revelation and the living Christ. These approximations are close to the divine model. In their outer aspects, of course, they *appear* very diverse. They speak many different languages. They wear many different clothes. They earn their living in many different ways. They have somewhat varying value systems. But at the level of revelation, above the superficial diversity, each form is drawing closer and closer to the Christian culture.

We can also truly say that there are many Christian cultures, for mankind is constitutionally diverse and the one way taught by Christ requires unity *in diversity.* All cultures in which Christ is Lord and obeyed are being purified and built into one temple of the living God, but they remain different substances — marble, wood, steel, and gold, perhaps.

To the Christian faith with its one way, Christian missions are neither arrogant nor impertinent. Rather, they are a humble sharing of the best things of life, often at great cost to him who shares, and never with hope of personal gain. Christian missions are not useless, as they appear to believers in cultural relativism, but a most valuable element in the life of the world. Far from being an imperialism devoted to self aggrandisement, Christian missions are the best possible service to sister peoples. Were we in their places and they in ours, we would want them to come to us with the good news of what God has done for men.

III   *Christians' Estimates of Cultures*

Christians look at Christianity and cultures in relation to God's revelation of himself in the Bible, in Jesus Christ, and in the present actions of the Holy Spirit in the lives of believers and the Church. Christians therefore hold positions similar to the following:

1. Cultures are the creations of men. To be exact, they are the creations of human societies, families, kindreds, clans, tribes, and classes of men who live together long enough to develop a distinctive language and way of life. Anthropologists with one accord declare that cultures are the creations of men. Men of science are unwilling to allow for any action of God in human affairs. Science describes only what can be seen and measured.

Men continually change cultures. They add something new and deduct something useless or outmoded. They judge this component of culture good and that bad. They destroy the bad without compunction and multiply the good and seek to make it better. Each society has its approved ways of making innovations. It is difficult today to find a culture anywhere on earth not in the midst of flux. Seething change marks culture, and the changes are made by men.

2. Christians believe that God has nevertheless played a part in creating the cultures of men. He created man in his own image, and though man defaced the image, he did not erase it. God gave man free will and enormous creativity. He placed curiosity and imagination within his mind. He gave him a perpetual restlessness with his achievements. God further gave man dominion over all things, to be used for the benefit of human society. And finally, (a) God gave all men a degree of revelation — the general revelation to which reference has been made — and (b) "what the law requires is written on their hearts" (presumably by God). God has continued to speak to this day.

Thus with some degree of guidance by God each tribe and tongue and kindred and *ethnos* has developed a language and way of life that fits its climate, resources, technology, education, history, and neighbors. And again, with some degree of guidance, every society goes on developing and changing and adjusting its culture to the ever changing circumstances.

3. However, man has steadily seen the good and done evil. He has known of God's invisible nature and power and deity — and made idols of men and beasts and reptiles. He has known that kindness is better than cruelty—and has been inexpressibly cruel. Consequently, the part God has actually played in cultures has been limited. We cannot entirely rule out God's influence on cultures. Directly and indirectly, God spoke to men as they created their cultures; but when we see what has eventuated — a tremendous mixture of good and bad, with the good always permeated with the bad, and the best devices of man producing unfortunate results (scientists splitting the atom and producing the bomb, the high feelings about marital fidelity in India producing widow burning) — Christians are confident that not much of the total process of culture making can be ascribed to God.

Of course, God is Sovereign and often overrules men. He takes their sour notes and works them into a new harmony. He took the cross and made it a source of new life. Yet God has given men freedom. He observes men making golden calves and worshipping them for centuries. This does not mean that he approves of golden calves or has in some way *revealed* them to men as suitable deities, or that, for such as worship them, they are true deity.

From the point of view of reason, the worship of golden calves is foolishness. From God's point of view—the unified witness of the whole Bible — it is sin.

Christians have a healthy scepticism about how much of culture is due to God. Since man is sinful, his cultures are bound to be sinful. God's holiness and righteousness make it impossible for Christians to believe God is responsible for the cultures of all races. It seems much more reasonable and much more in accord with Holy Writ to believe that man — discovering, experimenting, conquering, exploiting, deceiving, wonderful and sinful man — is responsible. It is man we see creating both good and evil cultural components. Some of his experiments turn out well, some disastrously. As he creates cultures, man sometimes does what pleases God, sometimes what God hates, and always less than God's will.

4. When once an individual congregation, denomination, or whole segment of mankind consciously patterns its life after the revealed will of God, the Bible, and allows the Holy Spirit free course in its daily affairs, then culture marches to a new drum beat. The more rigorously it follows the Lord Jesus and patterns itself after biblical revelation, the greater part God plays in its culture. He continually seeks to influence it without abrogating the free will he has granted man. In Jesus Christ he has given the perfect measure. In the Church, the body of Christ, he has given an incarnated means by which his will for each culture may be made known and made effective. In the written Word he has revealed his will. As men of each culture become disciples of Christ and responsible members of his church, feeding on his Word and measuring themselves by his revelation, the culture they have inherited and are changing and transmitting moves closer to God's will for it. It still makes mistakes — some of them horrendous — and commits sin, yet it strives after the divine model. The process can be seen in hundreds of Christian cultures in all six continents.

5. The Triune God judges all cultures, including the Christian. Like all man's fabrications, Christian cultures remain under God's judgment. They are better than they would have been had many of their members not become responsible disciples of Christ, but they are still far from perfect.

6. Since each Christian culture fits a different geography, climate, technology, economy, and heritage, the changes it makes as it discovers God's will for it will *not* transform all cultures gradually into one uniform model. For instance, a Christian

Japanese culture will, in many of its components, be very un-like a Christian Zambian culture. However, in many other com-ponents, a Christian Japanese culture will be very like its Zam-bian counterpart. In dress, diet, discipline, language, and form of houses and gardens (all neutral components), great dissimi-larities will exist; whereas in love for the Lord Jesus, obedience to the biblical revelation, what is regarded as sin and what as righteousness, hope of heaven, and many other such matters, great similarities will exist.

IV *Three Concluding Thoughts*

1. The clash between cultures and Christianity which I am describing has differences and similarities to that which Richard Niebuhr discusses. He treats of *Christ* and culture and says, "The debate . . . is not essentially the problem of Christianity and civilization, for Christianity, whether defined as church, creed, ethics, or movement of thought, itself moves between the poles of Christ and culture." [2] But I am talking precisely about Christianity, the embodied religion. Furthermore, he deals with culture in the singular. While he recognizes its pluriform nature, the myriad cultures do not seem vivid to him. Though he recognizes and rejects religious relativism, he is not troubled about it. Then too, while he maintains that "Christ" is the ultimate authority, he does not tell us clearly how we know this. He says: "The power and attraction Jesus Christ exercises over men never comes from him alone, but from him as Son of the Father . . . as man living to God and God living with men." [3] Or again, "He does not direct attention away from this world to another; but from all worlds present and future, ma-terial and spiritual, to the one who creates all worlds, who is the Other of all worlds." [4]

Niebuhr never mentions the Bible as authority. On the con-trary, I discuss Christianity and cultures in the light of the

Bible, God's infallible Word to the human race, in which are all things needed for faith and practice.

Despite these differences, I am indebted to Niebuhr's far ranging treatment of the topic. He describes five possible convictions which men might hold about Christ and culture; namely, Christ is against culture, Christ is of culture, Christ is above culture, Christ and culture continue on in paradox and tension, and Christ is the transformer of culture.

The point of view I am advancing has much similarity with the last. I agree with Niebuhr when he says that the men who hold this view

> belong to the great central tradition of the church. Though they hold fast to the radical distinction between God's work in Christ and man's work in culture, they do not take the road of exclusive Christianity into isolation from civilization or reject its institutions with Tolstoyan bitterness.[5]

2. The standardless pluralism which forms the first of the opposing forces I have described is a new development for the West, where for a thousand years Christianity was the only religion and its way the only way.

Yet standardless pluralism is an old story to the human race. The New Testament churches multiplied exceedingly in a welter of religions and ethical systems, in the midst of myriad cultures and languages. Easy tolerance for many cultures and gods marked the Roman world, provided only that incense were offered to Caesar (more a political than a religious act). The tremendous civilization of India rose on the axiom that mankind exists in a multitude of different castes, each of which has its own god given *dharma* or lifestyle. Righteousness consists in following one's own lifestyle. Each inferior or *Shudra* caste follows its *dharma*, and each superior or twice born caste correctly follows its. In India, Christianity has always faced a pluralistic society built on religious relativism.

Standardless pluralism challenges not only the entire missionary enterprise, but also all Christian churches here in the United States and throughout the world. The clash between Many Ways and One Way is of vital significance to laymen and ministers as well as to missionaries. Indeed, Christians everywhere have such a large stake in the battle that they ought to understand what is going on. Christian colleges and seminaries should provide their students with a reasoned defense of the Christian position. Churches should educate their members in today's great danger.

3. The problem of the Many and the One exists at several levels. It involves the relationship of Christianity to other religions, and as such it must be studied and solved on philosophical and theological grounds. Yet since America today is acutely conscious of many cultures and lifestyles, and since the missionary enterprise meets the problem chiefly on the cultural level, I shall not deal primarily with the relation of Christianity to other religions. Rather, I shall explore One Way and Many Ways on cultural grounds. We shall discuss Christianity *and cultures*. What should Christians do in specific cultures in the West and East? Does Christianity necessarily change cultures whose members live as practicing Christians? When Christianity and cultures clash, which one gives way? How different will "Christianity" be in different cultures? As men in different cultures become Christians, what elements of their old culture will come into the Church?

These are some of the questions we shall be asking.

CHAPTER TWO

ILL DEFINED ATTEMPTS AT A TRUCE

No question faces the missionary with more insistence than what form Christianity should take when churches begin to multiply in a different culture. He faces the question not on a theoretical, but on an intensely practical level. If he gives the *wrong* answer, the church he founds will likely become a closed-off enclave of foreign religion. If he gives the right answer, soundly Christian churches will be more likely to multiply.

Since the clash of cultures and Christianity occurs wherever the Church is advancing on new ground, it is an old story to Christian missions. Mission thinkers from the time of Paul onward have spoken to it. The science of missions (missiology) has often addressed itself to the problem and pronounced on it. Innumerable attempts at resolving the conflict have been made; yet attempts at a truce between the warring parties, or to change the metaphor, adjustments made by both Christianity and cultures, leave much to be desired. Particularly those schools of missiological thought which, like my own, heavily emphasize the need to adjust to cultures must work out a solution which at the same time guarantees the integrity of essential Christianity.

Biblical missiology today affirms that Christianity *must fit the context and make adjustments to each culture into which it flows while remaining true to its God-given revelation.* Throughout these chapters, I shall be exploring the implications of this double affirmation. In this chapter, adjustments will be observed from four points of view.

I   Adjustments Made Across the Centuries

In the long expansion of Christianity, many adjustments to culture have been made. When Martin Luther was born, the Church was a conglomerate of New Testament Christianity and many cultural accretions which it had picked up along the way. Among these were the celebration of the birth of the Lord Jesus in December and the use of the Christmas tree. As the Presbyterians in Scotland sought to get back to primitive Christianity, they strictly banned the observance of Christmas, rightly affirming that there are no biblical grounds for it. Christmas and the Christmas tree are adjustments which Christianity made to pagan religion.

As the Spaniards conquered and baptized the Indians in Latin America, they commonly gave the names of saints to mountains the Indians had worshipped as deities. Roman Catholics also built churches over Indian holy places, believing that the Indians would thus come without resentment to worship in a Christian fashion. In practice, however, since Indians were left illiterate and denied knowledge of the Bible in their own tongue, this policy did not lead them to become good Christians. Millions of Indians continued worshipping the old gods. They were really Christo-pagans. The adjustment encouraged syncretism rather than introduced Christianity.

Jesuit missionaries in China between 1600 and 1700 worked out a somewhat similar adjustment in regard to worship of the ancestors. They proposed to allow bowing to the ancestral tablet, provided the ancestral tablet for Christians clearly stated on its face that the worship offered before it was of the Triune God.

After a century of controversy between the Jesuit missionaries and the papal authorities, Rome declared the adjustment unacceptable. I am told, it has recently been coming back into Roman Catholic practice in Taiwan and other lands.

In the twentieth century we find very wide acceptance by Protestants and Roman Catholics alike of the exterior forms of multitudinous cultures. Drums are regularly used in Christian worship in Africa, and *tabalas* and hand harmoniums in India. Indigenous dress is the rule in most African and Asian churches; indeed, as the West Danis of the Baliem Valley in Irian became Christians, they continued — with missionary approval — to wear their national costume: liberal applications of pig fat and powdered charcoal, and nothing else! In the United States, cultural elements of the Jesus People such as long hair and bare feet have without difficulty been accepted in Christian congregations of counter culture people. In short, the clash has often been resolved by simply taking into Christianity a great many outer elements of the new culture.

All around the world, churches are being built in hundreds of thousands of villages strictly according to local styles of architecture. In towns and cities, however, church buildings still appear western; after all, a church seating hundreds of men and women in all kinds of weather is no part of most existing cultures. The only models are western models. Some Christian architect would confer a lasting benefit on the Church if he would devote ten years of his life to designing, in a hundred different locations, models of churches which use local cultural artistry, are economical to build, enable Christian worship and education to continue rain or shine, and are reasonably durable.

Black churches in the United States show clearly how Christianity has adjusted to culture. For two hundred years, while the vigorous biblical Christianity of the North was gathering its strength to demand the emancipation of the slaves, blacks became Christians in churches copied after those of the dominant whites. The Christian slaves were of course terribly handicapper in their effort to produce Christian churches. The low-grade Christianity which took shape was an adjustment to the slave culture. Marital laxities which slavery forced on the black community, though strictly condemned in the Bible, had to be accepted as part of "black Christianity." In this case, to the shame of whites and the impoverishment of blacks, culture won out over Christianity.

Today as black culture in the United States is breaking out of its chains, books are being published on "black English" which preachers should use, and "black theology" which they should teach. Black leaders are rightly advocating that Christianity make adjustments to their culture, saying that Caucasian Christianity is a mixture of affluence, white dominance, inherited privilege, sex standards which suit white Americans, *and* essential New Testament Christianity. They are demanding a different mixture in which New Testament Christianity is joined to poverty, black pride, hatred of oppression, sex standards which suit blacks, and a fierce thirst for justice.

Missiology, which meets this same challenge abroad in a thousand guises, is inclined in many particulars to vote with the blacks. Since black Christians live in a black culture, the Christianity they practice already fits many of its components and must be made to fit more. Biblical Christianity has no difficulty making adjustments to black idiom and thought forms which build up in Christians a desire to live justly and to oppose oppression.

II *Adjustments Which Should Not Be Made*

As Christianity flows into new cultures at home and abroad, it has no real difficulty making adjustments which accord with the plain meaning of the Scriptures. Christianity loves adjustments calling for greater justice and opposition to oppression.

In such cases adjustments are made in harmony with what the Scriptures teach.

But Christianity strongly objects to making adjustments which violate essential Christian teachings. For example, Christianity refuses to accommodate to sub-Christian sex standards whether advocated by whites or blacks. In the case of adjustments to black culture, missiology would argue that Christians err if they suppose the lax marital standard which slavery forced on blacks is a desirable part of black culture. Christian blacks, even more than black Muslims, should reject it vehemently. The only sex standards Christianity knows are those clearly set forth by Christ.

Two black legislators in Maryland recently proposed a new law requiring that marriage in Maryland be a three year contract renewable if both parties desire. They may very well have believed that such a form of marriage fits contemporary black culture.

In Jamaica, the huge majority of working class blacks practice what they call "The Jamaican Way of Marriage," in which men and women form temporary unions at will. Some unions last a week, others a month, some a lifetime. All denominations in Jamaica, from Anglican to Pentecostal, rule that men and women living in "The Jamaican Way" may not be members. Hence the vast majority of working class Jamaicans, though they count themselves Christians, are out of the Church. When a man and woman have lived together for years and reared a family, they may, if so inclined, get married. Christian marriage to them is a status symbol which means: "These persons are affluent, can afford a big wedding, and will now become-members of some church."

In both Maryland and Jamaica, the argument that since Christianity must fit the culture it must accommodate itself to fornication meets with a solid "No" from Christians. At the same time, missiologists are quick to say that Christian marriage in Jamaica must cease to mean a costly European affair (complete with gown, ring, wine, and flower girls) possible only to those members of the masses who have prospered in business. Christian marriage must be possible for poor men and women of the masses who intend to live according to Christ's command.

Adjustments should harmonize with the plain meaning of the Bible for an additional reason; namely, that they so easily become excuses for keeping oppressed peoples oppressed. This is beautifully illustrated by the Laws of Manu, which were the supreme legal code for Hindu India for over two thousand years. These teach that each culture must remain itself. The upper castes, for example, must not force their brand of religious teaching on the Shudras. Shudra religion fits the Shudras. They must not be taught the Sacred *Shruti* of the upper castes. I have myself heard Brahmans say, "Gross idolatry and bloody sacrifice of pigs and chickens *feels good* to the low caste. It is abhorrent to *us;* but it would be sinful and quite useless to try to teach our high religion to these souls in a low state of development. You Christians do try to teach your religion to them, but you are making a great mistake."

Christianity can have no part in such glorification of cultural differences; or, to be more exact, such a skillful use of the dogmas of cultural relativism to advantage the powerful and to keep the weak perpetually ignorant. Christian concepts of the infinite value of each person reject emotional pleadings that backward peoples "must be allowed to remain backward. Really you shouldn't call what they do 'backward'. In their culture, 'backwardness' feels good to them and is therefore right for them." The best, Christians hold, is none too good for men made in the image of God and redeemed by the blood of Jesus Christ.

A seminary dean recently said to me, "I am all for making adjustments so that Christianity and our courses will fit the blacks studying here. But I cannot agree that since at its present state of development black culture allows and rewards undisciplined minds, therefore we give degrees to men with undisciplined minds. Degrees from this seminary mean that their holders are men — of whatever race — with disciplined minds. Black culture is no doubt deficient in systematic biblical knowledge—but we do black culture no favor in perpetuating that ignorance."

One frequently hears that Africans think in pictures and stories. Abstract concepts and closely reasoned generalizations suit the Greek mind, not the African. Christianity must not accept this dictum. A nicely-honed true generalization is too useful a tool to deny Africans the rigorous practice needed to master its use, on the dubious grounds that 'true generalizations' are no part of their cultural heritage. The argument is too close to the easy error a Belgian governor expressed to me in the Congo in 1954 when he said, "These Congolese are not up to self—government. Remember, they are just down out of the trees."

Christianity must object to any adjustment to a culture which will keep its adherents from sharing in the best knowledge, the best religion, and most powerful tools available to men today. The biblical principle that we are all one in Christ must be preserved in making adjustments to culture.

Whenever cultural adjustments are proposed which involve disobedience to God's revealed will made known in the Bible, they must be rejected. For example, the counter culture people together with many other pagan Americans are developing a lifestyle in which open, pre-marital sexual intercourse is a chief ingredient. Professors of sociology in hundreds of American colleges are prescribing as required reading books like *The Family in Search of a Future,* and *The Family in Transition.*

The latter contains a chapter by Duane Feld and Michael Gordon entitled "Mate Swapping: The Family that Swings Together Clings Together," in which it is stated that "mate swapping is an activity which involves common planning and preparation and provides subject matter for conversation before and after; thus it could further consolidate the marriage." [1]

A girl from the hippie culture was delivered of a baby boy in an Oregon hospital. When asked who the father was, she replied, "I don't really know. This baby, you see, has been a kind of community project."

The clash between Christianity and cultures affects all Christians. We are not only asking how the missionary can remain Christian while being sensitive toward the cultures he evangelizes, and pleading for an understanding of other cultures; but we are dealing with a problem which faces most Christians today. It is clear that Christianity can neither spread nor endure unless it recognizes that, while many can be welcomed, *some adjustments to cultures must be rejected.* That a custom is "part of a given culture" is not sufficient reason to incorporate it into Christian practice. It must also be agreeable to the Christian revelation.

III   *Are Early Erroneous Adjustments Permissible?*

As the Church expands on new ground, it continually makes adjustments to the culture it finds there. Some are good, some are not so good, and some are in error. Let us see several adjustments made in the New Testament churches and in Germany as it became Christian.

As the common people among the Jews came flooding into the Church in the years following Pentecost, they came as Jews. They continued going to the temple; they continued circumcising boy babies, banning pig meat, and observing Saturday as the Sabbath. To it they added a gathering on Sunday, the day the Lord rose from the dead. And they evangelized only Jews (Acts 11:19). Thus one-race congregations arose by the dozens; perhaps by the hundreds.

Dr. Everett Harrison in a letter to me writes:

> The manner of life of the apostles and their converts in the city of Jerusalem involved no breach with Judaism in such matters as circumcision, fasts, tithing, maintenance of the dietary regulations of the Levitical code, observance of the stated seasons for prayer and attendance on the great national festivals. . . . This policy was instrumental in facilitating the winning of a large company of the priests to the faith. . . . That Paul should be sharply critical of men who had crept into the Church and were making of the gospel a new legalism should not be taken as indication that he had renounced his heritage in Judaism in every respect.

The five adjustments to the old culture I have mentioned — temple worship, Sabbath observance, circumcision, food taboos, and limiting evangelism to 'our own race' — were at first allowed by the Church and then later ruled erroneous and gradually abandoned. However, from this it should not be argued that they were wrong for those first Christians at that time, under those cultural circumstances. Paul ruled clearly that Jews should not seek to remove their circumcision. He did not command Jewish Christians to refrain from circumcising their boy babies. Evidently some early adjustments, which later were omitted, were permissible for the time being. Most of the Jewish law concerning the Sabbath was transferred to *Sunday* observance, to the great benefit of biblical Christianity.

Similarly, as the Germanic tribes became Christian, they brought with them many pagan customs; or, we may say, the Church made some beginning errors in adjusting to the local cultures. Latourette mentions a few of them as follows:

> Yet some direct continuation [of pagan customs] there was. Wells held to be sacred by pagan cults were placed under the protection of Christian saints. The ritual connected with the wells and the acts of healing ascribed to their waters remained unchanged and were now ascribed to their new patrons. . . .

In Norway after conversion the old customary ale feasts were continued to insure peace and good harvests, but the ale was now drunk to Christ and the Virgin Mary . . . offerings were made to the dead on the fast of St. Peter's chair. . . . Pagan customs in honour of the departed [ancestor worship?] were transferred to that day [Feast of Souls] some of them with very little change. In Germany the fire which at the winter solstice had been lighted to Donar became connected with the name of St. John. Horses and cattle formerly under the protection of the gods of earth and fruitfulness were entrusted to St. Leonard. . . . Columba in his missions to Scotland is said to have substituted for the wands and charms of the pagans the Christian blessing and the sign of the Cross, and thus to have expelled demons. In pre-Christian days in Norway Thor was supposed to wage war against the Throlds, spirits of the mountains and forests. After the adoption of Christianity, the cannonized Olaf was substituted for Thor as their opponent. In Sweden in pagan days the image of Frey had been conveyed in procession around the fields to insure good harvests; in medieval times the shrine of St. Eric was brought to the same fields for the same purpose. . . . In Brittany many ancient mores, some of them apparently of pagan provenance, have survived woven into the texture of popular Christianity.[2]

We do not know how these erroneous adjustments were made. Did pagan leaders say, "We will become Christians only if our new God and his saints will provide protection from the Throlds, insure good harvests, watch over our cattle and horses, and ward off the evil spirits"? And so, to insure the movement into Christianity, did the missionaries make the adjustments? Or by that time had the Church on old ground instituted the practice of saints blessing fields and fighting off the spirits of forest and mountain? Did the missionaries simply say to the would-be converts, "Our saints protect better than your old gods. You will be under really good protection from the moment of your baptism"? Did ancestor worship come in because it was stubbornly carried on by the fearfully ignorant new Christians who threatened to go back to the old gods unless permitted to worship ancestral spirits? And so did the priest-pastors helplessly say, "Since you demand rites for your ancestors, we shall inaugurate a Feast for Souls on which you can worship them in a Christian manner"? We do not know the answers to these questions.

But we *do* know that, as in the New Testament Church, some early erroneous adjustments were corrected one by one across the years in direct proportion to the degree of biblical Christianity practiced. They were corrected even in those desperately dark and Bible-less centuries. And, of course, the Reformation, committed to the Bible as the only rule of faith and practice, swept away great numbers of such semi-pagan adjustments.

Missiology to date has been unwilling to allow any of the errors of the Early Church or other new churches to be repeated. The fathering mission must forbid all adjustments ruled wrong up to the present time. I raise the question of whether missiology has been right. Must not each incoming population, saturated as it is with its own cultural viewpoints, be allowed to make its own adjustments, even though we surmise that some of them will be in error? Should we not allow them to be made, confident that the Bible and the Holy Spirit will in the course of the coming years correct them?

These are delicate questions. The answers are by no means clear. For one thing, the power of the missionary to allow or forbid varies enormously. Few missionaries stand at the beginning of new movements with enough prestige to control events. Most missionaries have influence with a rather small number of Christians, and these comprise a tiny minority of the social group in which churches are multiplying. Then too, will the Bible be available to these people in their own mother tongue? And will the Christians form a sizeable proportion of the population or a small persecuted sect? Perhaps most important, does the adjustment which seems erroneous to the fathering ministers or missionaries seem erroneous to the new congregations? No adjustment should be encouraged which new Christians see as a deliberate worshipping of other gods. The cause of Christ is not furthered by teaching new Christians to treat biblical authority with scorn. But suppose the adjustment seems *right* to the new congregations *on biblical grounds?*

For example, as Christianity liberated tribes in Northern Europe into the glorious freedom of Christ, one of the adjustments insisted upon was that converts stop eating horse flesh, a favorite meat of European tribes. The biblical grounds for this are clear. The Mosaic law states that only animals which cleave the hoof and chew the cud are to be used for food. Horses neither cleave the hoof nor chew the cud. On the basis of *that* Scripture, horse meat had to be forbidden. But there are other Scriptures. The Lord Jesus declared "all meats clean" (Mark 7:19). On the basis of *that* Scripture, which according to most hermeneutics has priority, horse meat could have been allowed. I am suggesting that adjustments which seem erroneous to the founders and probably will be eradicated in the years ahead may be allowed or even encouraged, *if they can be justified by Scripture* and if they help men make the difficult transition to the Christian faith. The one thing to safeguard is the authority of Scripture. Adjustments contrary to some biblical passages must not be made because the other culture demands them, but they *may* be made if other passages support them.

Some adjustments which seem wrong to the founding missionaries or evangelists might be regarded as temporarily permissible, provided the Bible is accepted as the sole authority. For example, the Iglesia Filipina Independiente, (IFI) numbering a million and a half souls, was a massive 1902 revolt against Roman Catholicism. The IFI nevertheless carried over in its daily worship practically the whole Roman Catholic liturgy – incense, images, Latin mass, and much more. In addition, it affiliated with International Unitarianism, had a rationalistic unitarian philosophy, and rewrote the Gospels omitting all the miracles. Then in 1946 the IFI sought apostolic succession at the hands of the American Protestant Episcopal Church. The Episcopal Council of Bishops granted the request, provided the IFI would adhere to the historic creeds, use the Episcopal Prayer Book until it made one of its own, and send its men to the Episcopal Seminary in Manila to be trained for the ministry. Some cultic customs which the IFI had brought over from Roman Catholicism and had devised to fit Unitarianism were erased by these three provisions; but many more continued to be practiced in the years following the reception of apostolic succession. The American Episcopalians reasoned that if the IFI was sound on those three lines, everything else of substance would gradually be brought into harmony with essential Christian doctrine. In short, American Episcopalians allowed many erroneous practices to continue, believing they would gradually be eliminated. In fact, they are being eliminated.

Professor H.B.I. Turner, an authority on African independent denominations of which there are at least five thousand, points out that (1) many of these denominations have beliefs and practices which seem to Christians of the older churches impossible to defend on biblical grounds; and that (2) the denominations which accept the Bible as sole rule of faith and practice are moving toward orthodoxy. The Bible, so to speak, straightens them out. The Holy Spirit and the Bible are living powerful forces. I suggest that the older churches may well allow some beginning adjustments which seem wrong to them, as long as the Bible is accepted as the sole authority in life and worship.

Some adjustments which seem wrong to us seem right to men coming in from another culture. They defend these on biblical grounds. Missions must often allow such adjustments. After all, we see many of them in Western Christianity. For instance, Congregationalism seems wrong to Episcopalians, Protestantism as a whole seems wrong to Roman Catholics, and refusal of the Friends Church to celebrate the Lord's Supper seems biblically indefensible to the Churches of Christ. Yet not many Christians read Congregationalists, Protestants, and Quakers out of the Church. They grant that they are Christians—not as *correct* perhaps as we are, but nevertheless, in view of their faith in Jesus Christ and the Bible, still *validly Christian*.

Furthermore, some adjustments which seem wrong to the fathering laymen or missionaries may be able to be filled with rich Christian meaning. Deciding to celebrate the birth of Jesus at the winter solstice — a pagan sacred time, and using a tree valued by the old religion — has turned out fairly well. How much poorer the Christian year would be without the rich devotional life of Christmas. Might not some treasured practices of other religions be similarly "possessed for Christ" and incorporated within the Christian cultus?

If the Lord tarry, Christianity will face hundreds of years during which thousands of homogeneous units will one by one accede to the Christian Faith. Segments of humanity will declare for Christ, accept the Christian way of life, and pour into the Church. As this happens, Christian missions should hold three positions firmly. First, they should hold a high view of Scripture, about which I shall speak in a future chapter. Second, they should leave judgment of details to the incoming church, as long as it accepts Jesus Christ as God and Saviour and the Bible as the infallible Word of God, the sole rule of faith and practice. Third, speed of discipling must not be reduced until all new members measure up to standards which seem reasonable to old churches. Paul's practice was to preach, baptize, instruct for a few days, weeks, or months, and *go away* leaving the new converts to the guidance of the Old Testament Scriptures, oral tradition about the Lord Jesus, and the beneficent influence of the Holy Spirit. Some congregations did what he thought they should not (witness Corinth), but he trusted the Holy Spirit and the Bible to correct them.

IV   *May We Declare Adjustments Acceptable By "Abolishing the Rules"?*

Perhaps the most serious challenge the battle brings is that which makes adjustments and declares them acceptable by "abolishing the rules." By "abolishing the rules" I mean ridiculing the doctrine of the Bible as God's revelation to all men in all cultures, and praising and teaching the doctrine that every sentence of the Bible tells us only how men of some culture understood God and man. In addition, advocates who abolish the rules assert not only that there are many different cultural patterns, but that God has revealed them. They push the clash between One Way and Many Ways onto theological ground. Looking out on the pluralistic world, these advocates see tens of thousands of lifestyles, declare that God himself has created these, and insist they are about equally good in all respects. This grounds cultural relativism in God. It affirms that the dignity of each culture has been given to it by God. All contexts therefore have approximately equal values. Cultural relativism which a few decades ago rested on the speculations of men is now declared to be part of the immutable order of things, part of the eternal purpose of God. Consequently, we must treat every culture with great respect. Some go so far as to assert that, as God has revealed himself to the ancient Hebrews in the Old Testament, so he has revealed himself to all the religions and ideologies of the world in their scriptures and writings. Let the religious writings of the world, they cry, be the Old Testaments, each to be fulfilled by Jesus Christ and his New Testament.

Influential Christians have recently been declaring "Christ was there before the missionary came." To this obvious truth one might add he was there before the dinosaurs appeared on the scene. But these Christians mean something else; they mean Christ was there revealing true religion to men, and this redemptive light can be found in all the religions and cultures of men. These Christians view cultures, therefore, not as human structures but as something which God has created and blessed. By this simple device, relativistic conclusions of humanists are elevated into Christian theological dogmas. Humanists are content to say, "The cultures of men are beautiful." Deviationist Christians press in to add fervently, "Yes, Christ, who was there before we came, has given these beautiful cultures to the various tribes and families of man. Hence each of them has *ultimate* value."

The pressures of the pluralistic world and the need to be friendly and appreciative to men of every tribe and tongue have pushed some sensitive souls over onto theological ground. There, impelled by the Western guilt complex, they propose to remove the great rock of offense — the biblical revelation which so clearly declares that God has made known his way, the One Way for all men. They remove the offense by the following two arguments. First, they assert that since the Bible was written in highly limited ancient cultures, it contains only a highly limited "word." Since God was speaking to men of ancient cultures and intending to be understood, he couched his message in the idioms, thought forms, and world views of those times, which are meaningless to men of other cultures and eras. As men meditated on God they naturally phrased their conclusions in their language and idiom. The 'message' had many meanings for them, meanings which we can recover if we know enough about those cultures, but not much meaning for us who are so far removed from those primitive days. Furthermore, God may not have said what the Bible asserts he said. The words, they say, are the words of men and the writings are human records set down and transmitted by men. Consequently, it is ridiculous to imagine that the ancient stories, annals, poems, and legal codes of the Bible have much meaning for us. Certainly they have no more than many other ancient traditions and writings.

The second argument goes thus: God has been revealing himself to men of other cultures in their institutions, cults, and customs, and in the stories and writings of their wise men. These fit those contexts far better than the Hebrew-Christian, teachings and lifestyles recounted in the Bible. The Bible may, of course, be called God's Word, but so may other oral and written records in each of the cultures of men. Thus we are not left impoverished with One Way, but enriched with Many Ways.

This double argument denies to the Bible any universal meaning and at the same time affirms divine inspiration for each culture. The clash of conviction which rages round this argument is crucial for Christianity. A similar clash took place during the first centuries of the Christian era between Gnostics and Christians. Then the arena was the Mediterranean world. Today the battle is global. Take for example the following writing by Francis M. Seely, a Presbyterian missionary in Thailand who was one of the three-man core in the Bible revision committee set up in 1952. He also translated text books for the Thailand Theological Seminary at Chiangmai.

> I regard the Bible as a record of one way out of many ways by which God has spoken to his people which includes all humanity. The way God spoke to the Hebrews and early Christians and the way they understood and expressed what they heard of God's word was necessarily conditioned by their culture and that of surrounding nations. I believe God has spoken also in Thailand through Buddhism. . . . So to me to 'teach' the Bible does not mean to teach in such a way that the Buddhist will accept the Christian expression of God's revelation and reject the Buddhist expression of God's revelation. To 'teach' the Bible to me means to give insight into what happened in that

particular cultural situation and why it happened, and how the Bible expressed these things for the culture in which it arose. It means to bring about an awareness of the complexity of truth in relation to various cultures.[3]

Seely apparently maintains, first, that the Bible is culture-bound; i.e., God was so limited by having to give his revelation in Hebrew and Greek that he could not reveal universal truths binding on all people in all cultures. Seely's second main thought follows closely from this, namely, that God has also spoken to Buddhists in Thailand (and Marxists in Russia?) so that their cultural light is as good for them as biblical light is for Christians. Seely takes culture very seriously indeed. He grounds it in God. To put it more exactly, Seely believes that God *revealed* nothing and men perceived (manufactured?) many concepts which fit their circumstances.

Francis Seely is by no means alone. Many avante–garde Christians deny the doctrine of an inspired, authoritative Bible. W. J. Hollenweger, Secretary of Evangelism of the World Council of Churches until 1971, in his article *Flowers and Songs in Mexico* (IRM April 1971), assumes that cultural differences are so great that the plain meaning of the Bible will differ from culture to culture. "It may be," he says, "that Christians in different situations will confess Christ in mutually contradictory terms."

To Seely and Hollenweger, adjustments to various cultures present no problem. Since both adhere loosely to the authority of the Bible, they adjust easily to what exists in other cultures. Seely advocates taking over Buddhist forms because, quite contrary to what the Bible says about other religions, he blandly declares these forms have been established by God. Hollenweger justifies radical departures from the biblical norm because he thinks there is no plain meaning of the Bible universally binding on all cultures. The Bible is a pluralistic hodge podge of documents and means different things to different cultures.

Os Guinness is speaking of the same phenomenon when he writes:

> Without biblical historicity and veracity behind the Word of God, our theology can only grow closer to Hinduism. In fact, John Robinson's *Honest to God* and Paul Tillich's books are already read widely in India. One swami in Rishikesh pointed to *Honest to God* and said to me, "But surely your Western theologians are saying what we have been saying all along."
>
> Tillich asked at the end of his life by a student in Santa Barbara, "Sir, do you pray?" replied, "No, I meditate." The reason is obvious. Liberal theology has no propositional content, no verbal revelation; theology is only what *man* thinks about God — not what God has said about Himself and about man.[4]

To interpret the Bible in this way is to abolish the rules and to affirm that when the Bible says "Thus says the Lord" the only possible way to understand it is in terms of what men in that culture at that time conceived or perceived.

Abolishing the rules, asserting that the plain meaning of the Bible differs from culture to culture, and dogmatizing that God has spoken in Buddhist, Moslem, and Confucian cultures as definitively as he has in Christian, generates an extreme and dangerous form of the clash. Such deviationist thinking forms a sizeable part of today's missiological pronouncements. Similar concepts have become fashionable in wide reaches of the Church. They would have been acceptable to William Hocking, the Harvard professor who headed the Layman's Enquiry of forty years ago. His findings, unanimously rejected in 1933, would be widely accepted in 1973. He would carry with him many leaders of the World Council of Churches and some missionaries in the older boards. A significant number of western-educated leaders of Asian and African denominations also have deified culture to such an extent that "abolishing the rules" seems agreeable to them.

Summary

In this chapter I have portrayed four kinds of adjustments which have been and are being made, and asked, "Are these defensible?" The central question is: *How can we incorporate different cultural patterns in Christian life while remaining soundly and biblically Christian?*

CHAPTER THREE

FOUR IMPORTANT ASPECTS OF THE CLASH

As we press forward seeking to understand the correct relationship between Christianity and cultures, it is necessary to focus attention on four major aspects of the battle.

I *What The Battle Is Not*

A. The Western guilt complex, which forms such a prominent part of missionary thinking today, is no part of the battle. Including it clouds the real issues. Christianity is far greater than the Western practice of it. Indeed, Christianity can well claim to be an Asian religion; the Jews were an Asiatic people, and the Lord Jesus never set foot in Europe. Huge Christian Churches exist today in Asia. In planting churches in new cultures, missionaries of Korean, Japanese, Nigerian, and Indian denominations meet exactly the same problems as European missionaries. Just as American Christianity must decide whether extra marital sexual intercourse advocated by American sub-cultures can be accepted by Christians, so Thai Christianity must decide whether *Tak-Baat* (offering food to the monks as an act of merit) and *Loi-Ka-Tong* (washing sins away by releasing on the river small floats containing gifts to the *phi* or spirits) are acts compatible with essential Christian teachings.

The issue is precisely not "Will Western pride allow African and Asian cultural riches to play a part in the Christian Church?" If that question were asked, the answer is simple—of course it will. But that is not the question. The questions we ask are far more complex. What are those biblical mandates which must be obeyed in all cultures? What degree of accommodation to thousands of cultures may be permitted? Is one degree of accommodation permitted if the whole people accepts Christianity and another degree if Christianity seems destined to continue for decades or centuries as a persecuted minority? Do men become Christian when they accept Jesus Christ as Lord and Saviour and the Bible as their rule of faith and practice, or is it necessary to add certain ethical achievements? Could pictures of Jesus Christ be used freely in cultures where idolatry was no problem, and forbidden where the dominant religion was highly idolatrous? In such questions, must judgment be based on common sense? Or on the authority of the Scriptures? Or on both common sense and biblical authority?

All these questions were being asked long before there was a Europe and will be asked long after America has disappeared as a nation. The real issues concern essential Christianity, not those embodiments currently found in Europe and America.
B. The clash is not exhibited by missionaries' misunderstanding other cultures. In teaching "Christianity and Culture" at Fuller Theological Seminary I often ask my students to illustrate the clash. They are quite likely to respond with instances where missionaries misunderstood customs of an alien culture or idioms of an imperfectly known language. Such misunderstandings certainly handicap the communication of the Gospel, but they are no part of the debate going on between Christianity and cultures about the correct relationship between the two.

Indeed, the debate is best exhibited when men (missionaries and others) *who understand cultures well* differ about whether the Bible allows given adjustments and accommodations, or about whether the Bible or man's reason is the ultimate authority.

II   *The Clash Occurs Not With Cultures, But With Their Components*

Culture comprises tens of thousands of components. Each is an extraordinarily complex aggregate of many different ways of thinking, feeling, speaking, and acting. Most of these ways are determined by the climate and geography, the number of people who live in each square mile, and the state of the technology. Rice growing populations, for example, have an enormous number of cultural components directly dependent on rainfall, making rice fields, sowing, weeding, harvesting, storing, buying and selling rice, and cooking and eating it. Peoples who live by oceans and along rivers have cultures minutely determined by their environment. Other elements of culture have to do with the language which has been inherited, whether it is written, has a rich literature, and is buttressed by a system of formal book-based education. Still other cultural components deal with the processes of manufacture. These may be the inherited skills of the weaver or the learned skills of the mechanic on an assembly line. Only a few cultural components concern religious beliefs and practices. Customs regarding relationships with family members, employers, employees, superiors, inferiors, and strangers, make up a much greater part of the cultural whole. The point need not be labored. The enormous number of separate components is obvious as soon as attention is focused on it.

I spoke of cultures as aggregates rather than as organisms because, while a high degree of interrelatedness is observable, the components are seldom essential to the culture. Most components can be changed or even abandoned without trauma. Indeed, hundreds of components are rapidly being changed all the time. The paddle gives way to the outboard motor, bare feet are shod with rubber tires, walking gives way to cycle riding, ruralites become urbanites, illiterates become high school graduates, and the black governors of Uganda decree that a tribe which formerly wore no clothes must now buy and wear clothes or go to jail.

Recognizing the composite nature of cultures helps us see the correct relationship between them and Christianity. Christianity is wholly neutral to the vast majority of cultural components. Let us take a specific instance. The easternmost province in India is Nagaland, a small mountainous section practically all of whose inhabitants belong to the fourteen Naga tribes. More than half the Nagas have become Christian and the rest are on the way. The Baptist missionaries who planted the first churches in the Naga tribes accepted without a second thought all those multitudinous aspects of the Naga culture which deal with how the people grow grain, cut wood, make beds, cook their food, entertain their relatives, and settle their quarrels. At least ninety-five per cent of the Naga culture came into the Christian faith automatically. Neither missionaries nor Naga ministers expressed themselves one way or another concerning this tremendous body of cultural components.

Christian Nagas worked at the same jobs as non-Christian Nagas. They built their houses in the same way, washed their clothes in the same way, spoke the same languages with exactly the same intonations, walked the same paths, and ate the same food from the same vessels. The Nagas brought their tribal way of life right into the Church, and enriched the Church universal with their distinctive life-style. At least with ninety-five percent of it!

What about the remaining five percent of the cultural components? These fall into three categories. Some components Christianity welcomes as particularly wholesome and desirable. Some Christianity changes and improves. And, on the authority of the Bible, Christianity declares that a few components are unacceptable to God and must be abandoned. While the three categories contain only a small part of the total cultural complex, they are important. We shall consider each separately.

a) Some components Christianity welcomes. The Naga custom of welcoming guests was recognized as good and incorporated in Christian practice. Numerous examples can easily be given from every area where the Church has flourished. Let me cite only one from my experience in village India. It is the strict custom of the Satnamis that when a member of the caste dies all his caste fellows in the vicinity gather immediately to dig the grave and express their sympathy for the bereaved family. As the churches formed out of the Satnami community, this cultural component was heartily welcomed. It guaranteed that at the time of death the new weak churches would rally together. Scattered Christians would support each other. Strong men would be present to dig a decent grave and to carry the body out to be buried. If anything, Christians gathered more faithfully than non-Christians, for they recognized this cultural component as a thoroughly good one.

b) Some components Christianity changes or improves. In the Naga tribes, youths were educated informally in the ways of each tribe and slept in a common 'boys dormitory', which had an elaborate social structure and system of government. When tribesmen became Christian, the youths continued to sleep in a (now Christian) boys' dormitory with the social structure and system of government largely unchanged. In addition, modern education was regularly taught in day schools. In the Middle Ages, as the warlike European tribes became Christian, the Church over a couple of centuries developed the institution of chivalry. Since abolishing warfare was impossible, the Church muzzled it. In most agricultural communities, peasant farmers need seed at sowing time. In pre-Christian days they borrowed this at exhorbitant rates of interest from seed lenders. The Church, recognizing this cultural component as essential but deploring the high interest, organized cooperative seed unions so that seed for sowing became available at reasonable rates of interest.

c) Some components Christianity declares are unacceptable to God and must be abandoned. Thus Christianity banned Naga head hunting. All around the world, as men become Christian, the paraphanalia of idolatry and spirit worship must go. Christians take the lordship of Christ seriously. The first command, "Thou shalt have no other gods before me," is clear. When all the Madigas in a village south of Bezwada decided to become Christians together, they took the idol out of their temple and threw it into the village pond. When James Frazer was called to a village in which the Lisu had decided to become Christians, he went round with them from house to house, and the about-to-be-baptized tore down the buffalo heads, paper shrines, amulets, and other debris of by-gone sacrifices, piled them in the courtyard, and set fire to them. Biblical precedents for such action are numerous; Gideon's first act when he became Jehovah's man was to pull down the image of Baal with his father's oxen.

We can now see the exact locus of the clash. As Christianity flows into the many cultures of mankind, there is no clash with ninety-five percent of their components; furthermore, there is no clash with the components which Christianity welcomes and those it improves. Clash is confined to one or two percent of the components.

Though these comprise but a very small proportion of the whole, they are important; they are the gods which have been worshipped, the fetishes which have been feared. Abandoning them is not easy. Converts must decide whether Baal is god, or Jehovah. As the long piles of fetishes and charms were burned at Pyramid Station in the Baliem Valley on the day when eight thousand clansmen declared for Christ, the flames consumed things which a few days before had been exceedingly precious. When a Hindu eats with Christians, thus breaking caste and putting a seal of finality on his baptism and his public confession, this single act carries a very heavy weight of emotion. This is what Alan Tippett has called the power encounter. He maintains that it is an essential part of becoming a Christian from another religious system. Dr. Tippett's idea is that when the would-be convert declares his faith in Christ, a power encounter ensues between Christ and the spirits or gods. The convert bets his life, as it were, that Christ will be the victor. At this point the Bible is clear, and all Christians (with the possible exception of a few left wingers who decry the need for conversion at all) maintain that Christians must worship Christ, who sits on a solitary throne.

Regarding attendant rites and ceremonies, however, there is considerable disagreement among both nationals and missionaries. Jesus Christ must be acknowledged as God and sole Saviour, yes. But!

Must ancestral tablets be burned? Confucius taught that bowing before ancestral tablets was an act of respect, but most people do it as an act of worship.

Must Christians refuse to partake of the Hindu death feast on the tenth day? Hindus hold that partaking feeds the soul of the departed.

Must Christians cease to feed the Buddhist monks? Buddhists teach that doing this accumulates merit and helps the soul along the path to Nirvana.

Must Christians cease bowing at the Shinto shrine? This act is held by some to be no more significant than saluting the flag, but by others to be worship of the spirits.

In caste conscious India, must Christians of any caste eat with Christians of other ethnic background and partake publicly of the Lord's Supper? This one act breaks caste and cuts them off from their own people as effectively as death.

Among the Nuer, a Nilotic tribe in West Ethiopia, the rite

by which a boy becomes a man consists of heavy cutting and scarification of the head, a bloody business which, however, has no spirit worship connected with it. Does becoming a Christian necessitate refusing to be thus marked?

In all these examples, the questions are: *which elements of the old religious system* (which shades off into a social system) *properly accompany becoming a responsible member of Christ's Church? And which must be forbidden?*

Furthermore, what is *the authority* which determines the answer? Is it customary practice in the founding church? Or the judgment of a budding anthropologist? Or the consensus of opinion among the recent converts? Or the practice of the Early Church? Or the experience of church leaders (nationals and missionaries) as to what, under those particular circumstances, actually does most benefit the church? We shall pursue these questions later on. Here it is sufficient to observe that, whatever the answer, the clash we have been studying is not with the context as a whole, but with those elements of it which require or symbolize allegiance to another god, another saviour, another scripture, or a significant part of another religious system.

III   *Is the Clash Necessary Because Breeds of Men Are Different?*

One continually hears that men are essentially different, therefore different cultures have different value systems, men of one culture have difficulty understanding men of another, what is right for one culture is pronounced wrong in another, and as a result there *cannot* be one revelation for all men. Is this really true? Or are men basically the same and is truth the same for all men?

A remote Amazonian tribe practices cannibalism. Non-Christian Nagas raid the Hindus to collect heads. Pagan Icelanders in A.D. 900 practiced female infanticide. High caste Hindus in A.D. 1800 thought it the height of wifely devotion for a widow to mount the funeral pyre of her husband. It has been commonplace for Christians to condemn such actions, but with the tremendous popularity of cultural relativism, voices are raised today to ask, "May it not be that, *for that kind of people, those actions are right?*"

At base, this question depends on how we answer another query: Do men come in different breeds? Whooping cranes are said to be strictly monogamous, whereas among cattle polygamy apparently suits them best — at any rate, one bull serves many cows. Are men similarly of different breeds? Do they have *biologically* different minds, abilities, understandings, and needs?

Many primitive tribes hold that other men are biologically different. They call themselves 'men' and use derogatory names for other tribes. Such thinking is not confined to primitives. When the Normans conquered the Saxons in 1066, they continued for more than a century to scorn the Saxons as an inferior breed. As late as 1939, a great nation and its scientists subscribed heartily to the theory that German Aryans were the master race. Americans, Hitler used to say, would never win the war because they had allowed intermarriage with many races and hence had debased the blood and mongrelized the race.

The best scientific thinking of the last fifty years, however, has come down solidly against the thought that races are different breeds and differ markedly in mental or physical abilities. Anthropologists who have long stressed the differences of various cultures are now emphasizing the basic unity of mankind.

Walter Goldschmidt, the anthropologist, declares that "people are more alike than cultures." [1] He sees world-wide similarities in dissatisfaction, selfishness, exploitiveness, conflict, and tension. He rejects cultural relativism, saying that it was a necessary phase in the development of the science of man but has now ceased to be useful.

Dr. Lloyd Kwast says, "It is precisely because all men are similar that God can address Himself in Scripture to all the *ethne* (peoples) of the earth. God intended to communicate His truth to the entire creation . . . . basic similarities make cross cultural communication not nearly so difficult as some would have us believe. The true, intended meaning of the biblical revelation as delivered to an ancient Hebrew or Greek culture can be clearly and correctly understood by Spirit-directed men in every human culture today." [2]

The innumerable minor differences between men in each culture and between whole cultures do not cancel basic human likenesses. God has, after all, made of one blood all who dwell on the face of the earth. Men are all descendants of Adam. All alike have sinned and come short of the glory of God. And, on that Day, all will stand before the Judge. Indeed, when we examine the matter closely, we see that the essential similarity between men of all races and cultures is so great that One Way seems eminently reasonable. In every culture, two and two make four, kindness is better than cruelty, contradictions cannot both be true, and love is better than hate. It cannot be that for some colors of men the earth is flat and for others round, for some God is personal and for others he is impersonal. True, some men have lifestyles built on fatalism and others have lifestyles built on free will. But it is absurd to reason from this that the biological make-up of the one requires fatalism and that of the other requires free will. It is still more absurd to conclude that in some mysterious way both a closed mechanical system and an open personalist system are equally true explanations of the way the universe is put together.

IV Four Kinds of Christianity Clash with Culture in Varying Degrees

In discussing the clash between Christianity and cultures, I have thus far followed common practice and used the term

'Christianity' in a loose, general sense. What Christians and churches believe, think, and do is commonly called 'Christianity' or 'The way Christians live'. But there are many different kinds of Christians. Some have high incomes, some low; some are highly educated, others illiterate; some are free, others slaves; some are members of episcopally governed denominations, others of loose associations of lay Christians. Compounding these distinctions are the enormous differences of language, geography, history, and technology. Furthermore, the way of life includes what people eat and wear, how they earn their living and amuse themselves. Truly, there are *tens of thousands of ways of life* practiced by Christians. As long as we define 'Christianity' in this loose sense, it is difficult to say anything intelligent about it.

It is helpful therefore to distinguish four kinds of Christianity. For the sake of simplicity, I shall call these Christianity One, Christianity Two, Christianity Three, and Christianity Four.

Christianity One is comprised of the beliefs concerning God, man, sin, Scripture, salvation, eternal life, and right and wrong. Christians necessarily hold these on the basis of the authoritative biblical revelation and the institutional forms of the Church which the Bible requires and the New Testament displays as the apostolic model. It might be called Theological Christianity. It varies slightly from denomination to denomination, but remains substantially the same.

Christianity One has a bearing on everything Christians do or think. It constantly reviews all components of each culture and seeks to bring them into harmony with God's revealed will. This remains true despite the fact that, under the pressure of many things, some newly emerging cultural components and some ancient accepted components alike get scant attention for years or centuries. For instance, in the nineteenth century, child labor and race prejudice grew strong before being challenged by Christianity One. In contemporary America, burial customs seem long overdue for review in the light of Christianity One.

Christianity Two is comprised of applied value systems — actions which Christians "ought-to-do-under-various circumstances." It might be called Ethical Christianity.

Christianity Three is comprised of church customs; ways of worship, forms of prayer, canons of song and praise, styles of architecture, and kinds of organizations. Everything which has direct relationship to the outward forms of churches and denominations is part of Christianity Three.

Christianity Four is comprised of the local customs of Christians. As far as sheer bulk is concerned, it is vastly larger than the other three put together.

The four types of Christianity accommodate to culture in varying degrees. Christianity One, comprised largely of principles and loyalties, remains unchanged in all kinds of cultural complexes. It readily becomes the new 'soul' in many cultures. It should be relatively little changed by them; rather, it transforms all cultures, both when it first enters them and throughout the years.

Christianity Two (what Christians ought to do in different circumstances) is considerably changed by culture. For instance, the Christian is commanded to honor his father and mother, but how to honor will be defined somewhat differently by men in different cultures. In some, it will mean obeying parents without question as long as they live; in others, it will mean occasionally visiting parents in a retirement home and writing to them often. As a second illustration, let us observe students standing when the teacher enters the school room. In some cultures this action is right; it means respect. In other cultures such a requirement would be wrong; it means not respect but subservience.

Christianity Three (church customs) will be significantly

changed by culture. In a highly literate, Bible reading culture, once a week worship with a twenty minute sermon may be a good custom, especially if Christians have many other opportunities for Bible study during the week. In an illiterate culture, daily worship in the village chapel after the evening meal is much more effective, and the Sunday sermon can profitably be hours long and cast in the form of question and answer. In one culture robes are in order. In another they seem ridiculous.

Christianity Four accommodates itself most completely to local cultures. When most missiologists talk about Christianity accommodating to culture, they are talking about Christianity Four. As far as ways of earning a living, dressing, cutting the hair, eating, and going about the business of life, Christians ought to follow their own cultural heritages.

But this is not always possible. When an invading culture has tremendous prestige (as Western culture had all round the world during the nineteenth and early twentieth centuries), many men, not merely Christians, 'go Western'. Then too, in the exploratory stages of the Christian mission, when the few who become Christians quite naturally attach themselves to the missionary — like Timothy attached himself to Paul — it is easy for Christians to become deculturized. In this exploratory stage it is difficult to prevent the first converts from becoming dependent on their 'father-in-God'. Timothy no doubt became much like Paul in the way he lived, dressed, and traveled. Yet most deculturization is a mistake. The new Christians should continue to look very much like themselves. Only so can they maintain close and affectionate contact with relatives and friends. The modern missionary has thought his way through the complex and puzzling relationships of culture and Christianity Four and is equipped to advise his converts how to remain in most of their culture while making those few changes which being a true Christian demands.

The adjustments and accommodations made in Christianity

Four are not always entirely right; but because they happen in Four and not in One, they do not destroy the Faith. Thus Sunday football and television in America are attended and observed by many Christians. Christianity Four has adjusted to them. Devout Christians sorrowfully accept such adjustments as inevitable at this time, confident that as Christians become more numerous and more obedient to the Lord, these adjustments of dubious value will be eliminated or transformed.

Much of the confusion which exists regarding Christianity and cultures could be avoided if those discussing the matter were to state which of the four kinds of Christianity they were speaking about. It is irresponsible to say broadly, "Christianity should accommodate to every new culture it enters." While that statement is true concerning many aspects of Christianity Two and Three and most of Four, it is not true about Christianity One. In this whole subject, as in most areas of life, exactitude is an ingredient of true thinking.

If Christians and missiologists would be punctilious in the meanings they wish to convey, many disagreements would be resolved. As we talk about Christianity and cultures, let us cease talking about 'contexts' and 'cultures' and begin talking about the specific components of cultures, which should be accepted or rejected by the Church as Christ liberates people after people.

Rachel Sweeting, writing from the University of London in a detailed account of many cultural components of the Gisu people, emphasizes the particularities involved:

> What, the Church has to ask, is "pagan" and what "just Gisu"? What of the Church's message stems from the "mores" of Western civilization and what is essentially Christian? The distinctions are vital. Upon conclusive answers to such questions as these depend not only the future of Protestant Christianity in Bulawesi but the nature and growth of the Christian Church in the whole of Africa.[3]

Let us cease speaking of 'Christianity' and begin speaking of the precise aspect of Christianity we have in mind. Considerable turmoil seems likely to accompany the liberation of the world's peoples, but turmoil damages advance and should be kept to a minimum. The evangelization of the world will be accomplished better if Christ's obedient servants avoid ambiguous generalizations and say exactly what they mean.

CHAPTER FOUR

TOWARD RESOLVING THE CLASH: PROPOSAL ONE

In the preceding chapters, I have explored the problem and touched briefly on elements of a solution possible to biblical Christians. In this and the succeeding chapter, I will expand these suggestions and others, and present a view of Christianity and cultures which honors cultures while cleaving to Christianity. My views enhance each culture in which Christianity is spreading. The riches of each will become richer and flaws will disappear or at least diminish. I trust readers, savoring the dimensions of the solution, will overlook the small degree of duplication inevitably involved. My proposals are three, of which the first will be presented in this chapter.

Proposal One
Let Us Take a High View of Scripture

In the uproar about cultures and Christianity which marks our day, discerning the right direction demands close attention to the doctrines of revelation and inspiration.

Much of the present confusion is caused by men who announce solutions to the problems of culture and Christianity without revealing their own position on these doctrines. Sometimes this is done innocently; sometimes, however, a man who

has abandoned belief in an inspired, authoritative Bible advocates an attitude toward other religions or toward the cultures
of men as a means of explaining how reasonable abandonment
is. Intelligent discussion of cultures and Christianity must be accompanied by a clear statement of whether or not the speakers
believe in the inspiration and authority of the Scriptures.
But more must be said than this. Most Christians claim to
believe in the inspiration and authority of the Bible; but they
believe it in different ways. Consequently, their clear statement
must also describe *the way* in which they believe in the Bible.
Their doctrines of revelation and inspiration must be stated
before their pronouncements can be evaluated.

Many books would have to be written before one could
describe and classify the different theological, philosophical,
and linguistic systems on which are based the many doctrines
of revelation, inspiration, and authority currently held by men
who call themselves Christians. This small book cannot cover
that vast field. However, the doctrines can easily be arranged in
a continuum running from a high to a low view of the Christian
Scriptures. A brief description of the high and the low view
may be in order. While many variations exist in each, the two
main ways of regarding the Bible can be contrasted. Each has
a distinctive view of the relation of Christianity and cultures.

A. The High View of the Bible.

The high view holds that the entire Bible — the canonical
Scriptures of the Old and New Testaments — is the Word of
God. It is authoritative and demands faith and obedience to
all its declarations. It is inspired and infallible and contains
everything that is necessary to the faith and practice of Christians. Apart from the Scriptures we cannot know about the
eternal purposes of God or the hope for immortality, or the
victory of good over evil. The Bible was written by men in two
of the thousands of languages of men, and the words are the

words of men. However, since God inspired the authors, the words are at the same time the words of God. God was not limited by the words and understandings of the men through whom he spoke in those ancient days so that they wrote only what was agreeable to their cultures and understandings. Indeed, they often wrote what was disagreeable to and angrily rejected by their cultures. They wrote what God was saying to them and to us. God used a current language and a current culture, but was not bound or limited by them. The writers, while immersed in their cultures, were inspired and therefore not culture-bound.

The inspiration of the Scriptures is not just a hypothesis. It is a part of the essence of Christianity, like the deity of our Lord. Our Lord was perfect man. He was born of Jewish stock, circumcised on the eighth day, immersed in the language and culture of his people, and obedient to the law throughout his life. *But* our Lord was also perfect God — the Word made flesh. He continually revealed truths from God and told men nothing but what God had told him to say. What he said speaks to men of all ages and all cultures. Similarly, the Bible is both the words of man and the words of God. What it says speaks to men in all cultures as if it had been (as indeed it was) voiced especially for them. Christians of all tribes and tongues feed on the Bible and find it convicts them of personal and cultural sins, nurtures their souls, and builds strong ongoing societies. My esteemed colleague Dr. Geoffrey Bromiley of Fuller Theological Seminary, who holds a high view of Scripture, says:

> The main point about verbal inspiration . . . is not that the words are inspired rather than their content, but that there is no such thing as the one without the other. The biblical message does not consist of general abstractions which can come in all kinds of forms. It relates to what is said and done by God in the working out of His purpose of grace and judgement. It has the character of historicity, particularity. The verbal

form is part of this particularity. It may be true that at times what is said might have been put in other ways; but it is, in fact, put in this way. This is no accident of history. It is part of the story. The form is not expendable. This content is not to be had without this form. Verbal inspiration is very important. It reminds us that we are dealing with God's word and work in history, not with abstract truths or insights. It commits us to a serious reckoning with the humanity of the writers — this man, this style, these circumstances. It thus binds us to the proper work . . . of linguistic study, exegesis, translation, and interpretation . . .

Scripture was uniquely written within God's words and acts not merely to provide an authentic record but also to present God's message and claim with enduring fidelity and power. . . . Scripture has a unique reliability by reason of its nature, function, and origin. Inspired of God, written to tell of His saving words and works, employed by the Spirit, it has a reliability unparalleled among other works. . . . In its divine function the Bible has the absoluteness of divine authority. This does not mean . . . it is an infallible encyclopedia of all knowledge. It does mean that what the Bible tells us about God in His word and work is absolutely reliable . . .

Modern disciplines such as textual study, literary and historical enquiry, and biblical theology have a significant part to play in understanding and interpreting the Bible. If they cannot solve all problems, they do at least try to show with greater precision what the Bible is really saying, not according to an external rule but from within itself.[1]

The high view of Scripture does not worship the words, for that would be bibliolatry; but it does insist that "all scripture is given by inspiration of God and is profitable for doctrine" (II Timothy 3:16). The high view remembers that the Old Testament assumes throughout that here is *God's* Word. The phrases 'the Lord said', 'the word of the Lord came', and the like are used 3,808 times in the Old Testament.

In directing mankind, God does not limit himself to his written revelation. In addition he speaks to men today, but never in contradiction to what is already written: The Spirit of Truth helps us to discover *from the written record* the new light we need for our own day and our own culture. The Spirit leads us into all truth, not because there is new truth apart from the Bible, but rather because we need a new understanding of what God has already said in the Bible and of its implications and extensions.

B. THE LOW VIEW

The low view, on the contrary, regards the Bible not as revelation, not as propositional truth, but as a *record* of human insight touched in some vague way by God. God said something, the man of God had a flash of insight, he experienced a beautiful 'high', and then wrote down his own words and thoughts. If we know enough about the cultural and historical situation at the time of his 'high' (so the low view continues), we can form a shrewd guess as to what God intended. When we add that knowledge to other similar knowledge derived from other passages of Scripture or other writings, we can calculate what God would say to us today in our situation. The missionary facing new converts carries the process a step further and figures out what God probably would say to these new Christians in *their* cultural context.

In the low view, Scripture becomes the radio over which God speaks to the hearts of believers. The radio is not the voice. The Bible is not the revelation. Indeed, parts of the Bible are no doubt in error and these the Christian need not defend. Nevertheless, he does believe that when he reads the Bible devotionally, God in some strange way speaks to him in his contemporary cultural situation.

Those holding the low view of the Bible often go on to assert that the scriptures of other religions and the writings of the great ideologies are given or 'inspired' by God in the same way. God spoke to those men in their cultures and they wrote down what *they* understood. Their writings have truth in them, though they are probably not as effective in conveying God's mind as the Bible.

In the low view, the Bible has little authority and no infallibility. In fact, the low view provides a convenient philosophical base for a high view of *culture*. One might say it substitutes the infallibility of cultures for the infallibility of the Bible. It considers these (like the Bible, it would add) the outcome of a long period of interaction between man and man, or between man and his gods, or perhaps even between man and God. Who is to say that lifestyles are not given by the divine?

An Illustration From India

This yearning to justify "our lifestyle" has led Christians of many cultures to argue that "whether our lifestyle agrees with the Bible or not, it is given to us by God." The process can be seen everywhere. Let us look at India. For well over a hundred years, noted Christian Indians have attempted to build *Indian* theological systems out of the Anglican and Roman Catholic systems which had, of necessity, been transplanted and used there. Furious argument developed in the process. Thought divided into two sections according to whether it rested on a high or low view of the Bible. For the high view there is no other norm for theology than the Bible — unchangeable, ever valid, and neither irrational nor suprarational. Developments in science, philosophical enlightenment, metaphysical speculations, intellectual pilgrimages, and the religious history of mankind cannot change this norm. The Word of God is truth.

The low view considers its task to be to bring the Bible into a new harmony with scientific thought and philosophical insights from Hindu religious books and doctrines. Two illustrations of the low view will make its general position clear. G. C. Oosthuizen has stated the case well.

Chenchiah, a highly educated layman, expounded his views in many books and articles. In them, Oosthuizen says, it becomes clear that Chenchiah "has no confidence either in the Bible (especially the Old Testament) or in the Church." He rejects "the Incarnation in the Scriptural sense, so that Christ may easily be posed as the fulfillment of other religions and as 'the new creation' for them." He "assigned authority to Christ only in this sense. He rejected the interpretations of Paul, Peter, and the other apostles." Chenchiah "wanted to study Christ's significance afresh, untrammelled by the tradition, doctrine or dogma." [2]

In similar vein, M. M. Thomas, Chairman of the Central Committee of the World Council of Churches, in *The Acknowledged Christ of the Indian Renaissance,* quotes Chenchiah's own words:

> The broad view holds that the only fixed immutable absolute centre of Christianity is the fact of Christ. . . . The other [narrow] view works with three absolutes of unchangeable core, unalterable faith, and essential deposit [all biblical].[3]

"The only fixed . . . centre . . . the fact of Christ" means that Chenchiah intended to cut Christ loose from the Bible — as Oosthuizen says. He then found "Christ" in Hinduism.

In effect, Chenchiah said, 'Back of the description of Christ in the Bible, lies the unknown Christ, the Cosmic Christ. The biblical description recounts how he was perceived by men immersed in Hebrew and Greek cultures. These perceptions are interesting but in no sense binding. The Cosmic Christ was also being perceived by the ancient Indian seers and scholars. Since we are Indians and live in Indian culture, our task is to perceive the Cosmic Christ in Indian terms. For us, these Indian perceptions are entirely valid.' Chenchiah intended to replace the apostolic interpretations of Christ, voiced in the New Testament which he held were culture-bound Greek interpretations, by Christ as he would appear in Indian philosophy. This inevitably eliminated the Gospel, an outcome which Chenchiah either did not see or did not fear.

Chenchiah is instructive because he shows with such clarity the inevitable result of assuming in the Bible a garbled, limited, culture-bound statement of eternal truths. If this is what it is, then obviously the Bible should not bind us today in Indian culture — or in any other! But Christians overwhelmingly reject Chenchiah's assumption, maintaining that the Bible is both the words of men and at the same time the Word of God. It was penned in the languages and thought forms of those ancient cultures; it voiced and voices God's will for mankind, for all cultures and all ages.

Chakkerai was another highly intelligent Christian wrestling with the problem of cultures and Christianity. "His contribution to theology was in opening the eyes of Indian theologians to the possibility of making Christianity indigenous in India" [4] in terms of Indian thought and culture. He reacted against Farquhar's position that Christianity was the crown of Hinduism, declaring that "the underlying assumption of these interpretative processes is that we know what Christianity is . . . all that has to be done to Indianize it is to give it a new intellectual form taken from the Indian religions and the Indian philosophic mind." [5] To Chakkerai this assumption was an illusion. He maintained that "Christianity is so badly misunderstood that we do not actually know what it is, so that one has to proceed *de novo* in India as in the West." [6]

Here again the basic thought is that the real Christ is not heard in the Bible. Rather, Christ is saying something behind or above it. Chakkerai allowed his pride in the Indian heritage to force on him — unnecessarily — a low view of the Bible. He derived his concept of and love for Christ from the Bible, for one knows nothing about Christ apart from the Bible. He then cut loose from it and projected a Cosmic Christ (strangely like the biblical portrait) fulfilling himself in every religion. Chakkerai never saw that if there *is* a Cosmic Christ not definitively revealed in Jesus of Nazareth, as described in the Bible, Hitler could have maintained that this Cosmic Christ had revealed to him the new Germanic religion and that he (Hitler) was the new incarnation.

Chakkerai was wrong about Christ, who reveals himself adequately and authoritatively in the Bible. About "Christianity," Chakkerai was partially right. Empirical (embodied) Christianity is always a mixture of culture and the pure biblical essence of the Christian faith. The Christianity Chakkerai knew in 1895 in India *was* heavily western in some of its aspects. Against these, Chakkerai's reaction was abundantly justified.

This is why I said his pride in the Indian heritage drove him *unnecessarily* into a low view of the Bible. Indian Christianity can and should divest itself of European cultural components by the score and should weave into its structure Indian cultural components by the hundreds and still remain biblical Christianity. Indeed, the high view of the Bible — taking the text most seriously — welcomes cultural diversity and rejoices in the cultural riches of every ethnic unit, up to a point. Chakkerai and Chenchiah did well to attempt to Indianize Christianity. The churches in India are in debt to them. But they did not need to advocate an undiscriminating unbiblical Indianization. Though he does not admit it, Chakkerai was really applying the Bible. He never, for example, advocated the ancient Indian lingam worship. He did not insist that goat sacrifice at the Kalighat in Calcutta be included in Indian Christianity. He did not advocate a standardless relativism or adherence to the Hindu teaching about *Maya Jal*. To these he applied the biblical norm.

The biblical norm must be applied to all of life. It will strain out of every culture what is detrimental to life and thus enhance every good and beautiful component. The high view of the Bible is the friend of Indian culture and every other culture.

The Low View Entails Agnosticism

Any low view of Scripture has the unvarying corollary that other value systems are equally authoritative. The low view defines right and wrong for *Christians* by what the Bible teaches, and for others by what *their* culture teaches. Thus we are left with a large number of differing lifestyles, all with strong claims to proximate validity and weak claims to ultimate validity. Together with this view that morality is relative and fallible goes the conviction that beliefs about absolutes (freedom, God, sin, immortality, salvation, and the like) are mere speculations. Since in the various religions these notoriously contradict each other, the conclusion readily arises that there is no sure religious truth. All religions are partly true and partly false. Their scriptures are men's thoughts and men's words arising out of particular cultures and of dubious validity in others. George Forell, describing the crisis in today's university, says:

> The current ethical crisis in the university is caused by the fact that many, if not most, of us no longer believe in any Truth with a capital T which can be attained by man either by means of theology or the most recent arrivals in the field of science.[7]

This is necessarily so. As soon as men cease to believe in a revealed truth — with all the difficulties which this belief entails — they gravitate irresistably and unavoidably to many perceptions of truth, each of limited validity. They cease to believe that the Truth can be attained by finite men. They become agnostics, though, as long as they are surrounded by true believers, their agnosticism is not apparent and its results are not immediately disastrous.

For example, Christians holding a low view of Scripture do so in the comfortable assumption that the truths of the Bible are well established. Low-viewers protest, "All we are saying is, we should not be too dogmatic about what we believe. Other religions also have much truth in them." Americans holding the low view speak in a country where "the truth of the Bible" is generally accepted. They do not see that, on the world scene, Christianity is a minority religion, and the low view of the Bible (when thrown into the arena with strong non-Christian religions and ideologies) must lead to the conviction that there is really no truth, no revelation, and, in the last analysis, no knowable God. The low view inevitably concludes that man's reason is the only real authority. Reason judges between the claims of different religious speculations. And, since reason fluctuates wildly, agnosticism accompanies the low view.

The high view of the Bible has difficulties, but they are fewer and less serious than those posed by the low. The first step toward a correct position on the clash of cultures and Christianity is a high view of the Bible.

In the view of general revelation which the Bible teaches, and the fact that God is the Father of all men and does not wish any to perish, the Christian must, I think, allow that God has shown men what he has desired. The first chapter of Romans says this clearly. But the Bible also declares in many passages that he came to his own and his own received him not. Though the light shone, men preferred darkness. They knew what God was like and deliberately made idols of snakes and dogs, penises and vaginas, and worshipped them. The Christian, granting that much beautiful, good, and true is found in the cultures and scriptures of mankind, cannot allow that any of these, or all of them together, are divinely inspired. The cultures and scriptures of the world contain too much that is trivial, gross, and absurd. As human manufacturers they are credible. As divine revelations they are incredible.

Is the Bible Part of the Supracultural? Or Is the Supracultural A Vague Something Behind the Bible?

A most important aspect of the high view of Scripture is

revealed by the two questions which head this section. They have been asked for many decades. Obviously, the difficulties posed by the Bible would disappear if we maintain that God's will is imperfectly revealed in it. If the Bible contains only the *human record* of revelation, the difficulties vanish. The argument runs as follows: God spoke to men, no doubt; but then men wrote down what *they understood*. What they understood was strictly conditioned by their language and culture, and so we should not be surprised that the Bible contains many things unbelievable today. It is not necessary for Christians to believe them. Rather, reading what the men of God thought under *their* circumstances, we can deduce what God really meant then and what he would likely say to us today.

According to this view, propositional revelation simply does not exist. The crude idea of God disclosing universal truths, and that the propositions in the Bible *are the revelation,* must be abandoned. Instead, Christians must discern in the biblical accounts and actions what God had intended to say. The Bible is not supracultural. It is, on the contrary, very much part of culture. Our task today is to study and understand the cultural complex in which the words were written long ago and deduce what truth lies behind them.

Christians who enter the lists on behalf of the Many Ways often hold a view of the Bible similar to what I have sketched above. Rudolf Bultmann in Germany, is famous for his version of this popular opinion. It is worth noting that his position is famous only because it gives classic expression to an enormously popular view of cultures. Bultmann stated clearly what that view of culture necessitated regarding the doctrines of revelation. He maintained that the Bible was strictly culture-bound. It used and was strictly bound by the myths of the day in which it was written. By myths he did not mean untruths. He meant stories, illustrations, thought forms, and scientific theories of that day. But, Bultmann went on, men's ideas change. Each era develops its own myths, its own way of expressing reality. Thus the Christian should ask, "What is the timeless truth which those ancient writers were seeking to express, and which (we might say) God was seeking to declare to those culture-bound people?" We study that culture, language, and technology to deduce what the essential meaning behind the crude forms was. We then express that essential meaning in forms intelligible to today's culture, language, and thought forms. *The hidden meaning behind the old myths is the only truth there is in the Bible.*

Bultmann was not speaking of translating the Bible. In translation it is of course necessary to discern the exact meaning of the Hebrew or Greek words and to express it as perfectly as possible in another tongue. Dynamic equivalents may correctly be used to state in this language what the inspired writer stated in that. But searching out 'hidden general truths' which lie behind the plain words is not translation. It is something entirely different. The Christian cannot accept as his only authority a vague supracultural Something which may be interpreted in a hundred different ways as the interpreter wishes. As Bromiley says,

> The biblical message does not consist of general abstractions which can come in all kinds of forms. It relates to what is said and done by God in the working out of His purpose of grace and judgement. It has the character of historicity, particularity. The verbal form is part of this particularity. It may be true that at times what is said might have been put in other ways; but it is, in fact, put in this way. This is no accident of history. It is part of the story. The form is not expendable. This content is not to be had without this form.[8]

It is essential to remember that biblical Christians, while declaring Bultmann in error, strongly affirm the need to understand the cultural and historical circumstances in which the books of the Bible were written. The force of Paul's argument in

Galatians is greatly enhanced by knowing the divisions and legalisms which characterized the strict Jews of his day and the missionary situation from which he wrote. Reverent inquiry into what the words meant to the men who spoke and heard them aids understanding of the Scriptures. But such inquiry must be carried on by men who believe they are dealing with God's Word as well as men's words. The meanings of the great passages of the Bible are so clear and applicable to modern and ancient man, black and white man, rich and poor man, that demythologizing is dismissed by most intelligent Christians. Far from helping men understand the Scriptures, it prevents comprehension. Elaborate search for general truths hidden in old myths is counter productive.

Preserve The Function: Let the Form Go?

As missionaries make empirical Christianity (the Church with its liturgies, organizations, institutions, and configurations) fit the myriad cultures of earth, they frequently make adjustments. For example, when the Alliance missionaries in the Ilaga Valley of West Irian first led the new Christians from the Uhunduni tribe to celebrate the Lord's Supper, they faced the fact that bread and any form of grape juice were utterly unknown to that isolated tribe. Uhundunis ate sweet potatoes. The only red juice they knew was squeezed out of wild raspberries. So Alliance missionaries used these two substances. The missionaries made adjustments not only in the practice of their churches in America, but also in the practice of the New Testament churches. They changed the *form* used in the New Testament while conserving the *function*. In a way, they grasped a changeless meaning behind a changing form.

This common missionary practice is to be commended provided the function *required by the biblical form* is preserved. Changing the form might easily impoverish or distort the biblical function and must not be allowed to do so. For example, if in some culture, memorial services were carried out by waving a white lily, it would not be permissible in the Lord's Supper to substitute waving a lily for partaking of a broken loaf. For "remembering the Lord" is only one of several key meanings of the Lord's Supper. Waving a lily might convey that meaning well, but not convey at all the idea of "the blood of the new covenant," or of the "body broken for you." Departure from either form or function as described in the Bible and demonstrated in the New Testament Church is as a rule unacceptable. The formula 'forms change: functions continue' is occasionally justifiable but must always be used in close conformity to the biblical norms.

Let us see what disregarding this principle might mean. Our Lord taught us to forgive our enemies. Suppose that someone, seeking to make Christianity fit a *dominant* culture, were to argue as follows: " 'Forgive your enemies' was spoken to a subject nation. The cultural context at that time made it expedient for those ruled people to forgive their oppressors. But in this dominant culture, the expedient thing is to liquidate enemies. 'Deal with your enemies realistically' is what God intended to say in the phrase 'forgive your enemies'; that is the hidden meaning which Christians in this culture should practice." The argument is extreme but legitimate. We immediately reject it because the meaning "discovered" behind the words (while eminently reasonable) is not what the words say. Furthermore, it does not harmonize with the rest of the teachings of the Bible.

The Church has again and again rejected symbolic or allegorical meanings alleged to lie behind the words of the Bible. The plain meaning of the Bible is the true meaning. Seeking behind the plain words for "new meanings which fit this new culture" opens the door to all kinds of subjective interpretations. The most notorious of these is that which blithely dismisses the resurrection of Jesus Christ as an idea obviously impossible to men living in this modern culture. It then interprets the plain statements of our Lord's resurrection as "the way in which the early disciples, living in that pre-scientific culture, explained their wonderful joy and power when they thought of the Lord as present."

The Bible is part of the supracultural as well as part of the cultural. Though given in the Hebrew, Aramaic, and Greek languages, it expresses timeless truth for men of every culture and every clime. As the Lord, the Second Person of the Trinity, was truly man and truly God, so the Bible is truly *the words of men* and truly *the words of God*. It is authoritative, inspired, and infallible. This is the high view, which is essential to any Christian resolution of the clash. Without the high view, the clash is far from being resolved; rather, it is made to resound more loudly. Without the high view, no authority exists. The culture that happens to be powerful at a given time spreads its way of acting and thinking, but soon falls and is replaced by another. Far from assuring the many cultures of mankind a fair deal, renouncing the high view simply delivers them over to the law of the jungle. Yesterday Assyria and Imperial Rome, today Europe and America, and tomorrow some other way of life. Today cultural relativism (what the other culture does is probably right) seems reasonable; but it did not seem so to American Christians in the thirties. Nazi culture seemed deadly wrong to them; a great war was waged to stamp it out. A few years hence some other world view may gain ascendency and force itself on men's thinking. The biblical revelation, which claims to judge both Hitler's worship of Germanic culture and today's worship of multitudinous cultures, offers a better chance that the *best* in each culture will be built into the emerging common value system of mankind.

CHAPTER FIVE

TOWARD RESOLVING THE CLASH: PROPOSALS TWO AND THREE

Proposal Two

Let Us Take A High View of Culture

Competent missionaries throughout the ages have tended to take a higher view of culture than the average trader, conqueror, or traveller; but a high view should now characterize all missionaries. With the insights of anthropology now available, a high view is easy to obtain. The low view can be readily recognized and ruled out. Ethnocentrism, which automatically despises things not done "our way," can be eschewed. National pride can be estimated as not always right.

Obviously, a high view of culture cannot mean that cultures are inspired, or authoritative, or in any sense one rule for all peoples. Cultures fit different physical, geographical, climatic, technological and educational circumstances. The enormous diversity of situations produces the enormous diversity of cultures.

The high view of culture regards each culture as *reasonable* given the specific circumstances in which it has developed. If one lives where eight out of ten babies die before the age of four and the average expectation of life is twenty-two years, it is reasonable to marry as early as possible and to produce a child every nine months. Nothing will better help the tribe survive. In a society which knows nothing of writing, the oral transmission of accumulated experience is given a high priority. Thus it becomes *reasonable* to lay great store on proverbs, stories, and genealogies. Under some circumstances, head hunting, the peculiar mythical justification for it, and the systems of rewards and punishments which encourage it, become *reasonable*.

Estimating the components of another culture as *reasonable given those circumstances* is not the same as judging them *right*. For the Christian, only what is in accord with the will of the Triune God for man, as revealed through the Bible and through Jesus Christ, is right. Furthermore, most cultural components cannot be measured in terms of right and wrong. Eating with fingers or with forks is not a matter of right and wrong; the high view of culture says to the Indian eating with his fingers or the Frenchman eating with his fork, "Excellent, but do it with the finesse which your culture demands."

Some components of culture have to do with personal relationships. For example, in some parts of India a younger brother's wife may not enter a room occupied by her husband's older brother. The low view of culture would be quick to say, "What nonsense! What a trampling on her rights as a person!" The high view of culture, on the contrary, would be quick to say, "Under these circumstances, where the older brother has a great power in the family, this custom is certainly reasonable. Nothing in the Bible requires us to abolish it. Rather, we should cherish it."

A high view of culture recognizes different ways of thinking and different systems of logic, knowing that these are equally good for conveying meaning — given the circumstances. Anthropologists often say that the ways of thinking effective in the West are poor vehicles by which to transmit meaning to men of some other civilizations having other systems of understanding reality. And this is true. Oppressed peoples, for example, habitually speak evasively. They use a system which they understand and others do not. For one thing, they use exaggerated agreement to convey indifference or even hostility to some proposal. Among themselves they know exactly what they mean, and so does the missionary who understands the system of logic being used. In fact, the competent missionary will himself be able to use the mechanism of exaggerated agreement to convey indifference. He learns not merely words and grammar systems, but also forms of logic and of humor.

It is common among new missionaries, who tend not to understand oppressed peoples, to scorn their system of logic and to maintain that it is no system at all. Sometimes it is charged that that way of speaking is not honest; it has built-in deceit. At this point, discriminating thinking is demanded.

Men do like to deceive others. The mechanism of exaggerated agreement to convey indifference, like irony or sarcasm, *can* be used dishonestly. Indeed, it frequently is, and when this happens it is wrong. On the other hand, when both sides know what is going on, exaggerated agreement to convey dissent is simply a form of speech, a kind of logic, a way of thinking which is neither right nor wrong. Like tall stories and vivid illustrations, it adds piquancy to speech.

The missionary who holds a high view of culture and seeks to communicate the Christian faith across cultural lines realizes he should know specific perceptual categories of varying relevance. Foods, which in the Western system are classified as carbohydrates and proteins, in the Thai or Indonesian systems are described in terms of cold and hot. Brown sugar is very hot, but white sugar is very cooling. Oranges are very cooling. So if one drinks a glass of orange juice with a spoonful of white sugar in it, he may expect to catch a severe cold, or perhaps get pneumonia. Hundreds of these perceptual categories must be known before one can operate effectively in another culture.

Now a nice question arises. Foods do in fact have different caloric values. A pound of rice has many more calories than a pound of cabbage. This is *true* in any culture. Whereas it simply is not true that white sugar is cooling and brown sugar is heating. This is *not true* in any culture. The high view of culture grants this; but in effect it goes on to say,

> Unless you are teaching a course on nutrition, you had better simply accept that a fixed component of the culture you are working with is that certain foods are cooling and others are heating. If you are planning a diet for a patient who is seriously ill, you had better not give him cooling foods when he and all his relatives "know" that cooling foods will be the death of him. Cultural components except in rare instances should be accepted as reasonable under these circumstances, even if they are not scientifically true.

So much for scientific truth; but what does one who takes a high view of culture do when a cultural component diametrically opposes the clear biblical directive? When such rare cases arise, the Christian has no alternative but to insist that the cultural component give way to the revealed truth. However, he would do well even here in most instances to encourage the Chritians to come to their own decision. If they are illiterate and, in the enthusiasm of their new found faith, want him to tell them what to do, he may have to make the decision; but he should make it clear that he is not proposing a requirement which the church of the West imposes on its members, but rather he is following a requirement which the Bible imposes on all Easterners and Westerners who follow its mandates.

It is impossible to exaggerate the need for understanding the different meanings cultures assign to activities which appear superficially the same. A high view of culture uses the disciplines of psychology, ethnolinguistics, and anthropology to gain more accurate understanding of meanings so that communication may be more accurate, biblical translation can convey meanings more precisely, and the propagation of the Christian religion in other cultures may be more Christian and more in accord with the revealed purpose of God.

Though taking a high view of culture, the Christian (missionary, anthropologist, minister, or linguist) needs to be on his guard at one point. He may truly affirm that since the book of Judges, for example, was written in Hebrew for pre-scientific man just coming out of the pastoral life of the desert, therefore the translator must seek to recover as closely as he can what the words meant to the author and to the listeners, and to state those meanings in current idiomatic English. He may not affirm, however (it is definitely *not* true), that those words (written primarily for those people and using so completely their thought forms and vocabularies, their systems of logic and grammar, their world views and perceptions of reality) have little meaning or authority for men living in the last quarter of the twentieth century. The terrible wickedness recounted in the twentieth and twenty-first chapters of Judges and the punishment which the Righteous God meted out to the men of Benjamin through his obedient servants the Israelites certainly had a meaning for men and women in that pre-scientific era; but the account also speaks powerfully to men today in every conceivable cultural situation. It tells of an eternal difference between right and wrong, of God who will not tolerate sin, who cannot be deceived, who counts righteousness as of greater value than mere extension of life, and who is so angered by sin against a helpless slave that multitudes of free men gladly went to their death. God's passion for justice and righteousness, embedded in this powerful story, is part of his continuing revelation. The Bible declares stern justice to be part of God's nature. Only such a view enables us to understand the cross. The cross would never have been required by a pale academic 'interest in justice'. Highly educated men who draw fat salaries and are "interested in justice" while never risking a picket line or a freedom march, will — if they but listen — hear God's voice speaking to them today out of those terrible chapters.

Ethno-linguistics is a tool which Christians with a high view of culture should use to improve communications with men of other languages. They should be careful not to use it to denigrate the authority of Scripture. Ethno-linguistics tells us how to translate God's Word effectively into the thousands of languages of men; but it does not state that men of a different culture cannot understand God's Word when the latter has been correctly translated.

God Commanded Men to Create Rich Cultures

Christians holding a high view of culture take seriously the biblical statement that God commanded men to have dominion over creation. As men carry out this mandate, ruling the rain forests of Zaire, the pampas of Patagonia, the high rise apartments of Singapore, the blast furnaces of Bhilai, and ten thousand other segments of God's creation, they generate rich cultures and lifestyles, each of which fits a particular environment. What an abundance of cultural riches! What creativity and free enterprise! The mosaic of mankind is a myriad of laboratories in which beautiful — and some ugly — patterns of behavior are constantly being developed.

God's purpose, seen so clearly in the history of Israel and the Early Church, was to encourage his people to take the riches of culture from every "kindred, and tribe, and tongue, and nation," and beautify the household of God. The Hebrews took learning from Egypt's palaces, gold from its houses, building skills from its construction crafts, and agricultural traditions from its fruitful soils. From the desert dwellers they picked up other gifts. Once in the Promised Land they learned how to grow grapes, tend olive orchards, dwell in walled cities, and cultivate fields. From the Philistines, David wrested the secrets of smelting iron and making iron weapons and tools. Solomon borrowed builders from King Hiram and beautified the great temple with the best contributions of the cultures of north and south, east and west. In truth, the wealth of the cultures of the world flowed into Jerusalem.

This is always God's purpose with his households; they should have dominion over his creation and multiply riches for themselves and others. It is his will that they should, even in the midst of evil, make everything they touch more beautiful and good and wise. With each Chosen People, his redeemed, with each *ethnos* he calls out of the land of bondage and takes to the Promised Land, God intends that the wealth of the cultures of mankind should flow into it. The diversity arising from human creativity as it meets the infinitely changing scenes of life is God-ordained and will be used by God. So declares the high view of culture.

At only one point is uniformity required — where the Bible indicates it. God's majesty, reality, righteousness, love, and way of salvation have been revealed and remain the same for all cultures. Man's nature, fallen and yet always able to respond to God's call for repentance, is uniform among all tribes and tongues. Each person in the world is called to glorify God. If any man on any continent in any culture will believe on God's only begotten Son, accept forgiveness, and walk in the light, he will be given the right to become a son of God. The truth that Jesus Christ died for our sins according to the Scriptures and according to the Scriptures was raised on the third day cannot be deduced. This supracultural truth is *given* in the Bible. God has revealed it. It is true for all races and conditions of men. The coming Kingdom and its foretaste in the Church of Jesus Christ are the same for all civilizations. All cultures will stand before the same Judge. The biblical revelation and the historical truths in it are exactly the same for all the clans and kindreds of men. Since these uniformities, which comprise the unchanging heart of the Christian faith, purify, beautify, and improve all cultures which adopt it, Christianity makes the richness of each culture richer.

These uniformities are not to be conceived in any wooden fashion. The written Word is always supplemented by the spoken Word. What God currently says through his Word, the light which the Holy Spirit constantly causes to break forth *from the Word*, will vary from culture to culture and from age to age within the same culture, and thus further multiply the possibilities of acting in ways which both conserve culture and obey God.

The first two parts of the way I propose to resolve the clash between Christianity and cultures involve holding simultaneously a high view of Scripture and a high view of culture.

Proposal Three

Let Us Allow Differences of Opinion

As the Church expands, adjustments in culture, even when made on biblical grounds, look different to different Christians.

Missiologists are well acquainted with adjustments to cultures. Theoreticians speak and write a great deal about them with much divergence of opinion. Practitioners (missionaries and ministers meeting new cultures in the churches) make innumerable adjustments, often in different directions! The process is continuous. It goes on in American cultures and in ten thousand other cultures scattered round the globe. The process is extremely complex. As we consider what adjustments may properly be made and how they may be defended on biblical and practical grounds, it will help to see several ways in which differences arise.

1. Differences arise because meanings change.

The meaning of cultural components differs with the context. For example, to my Scotch ancestors striving to free themselves from the cultural and doctrinal accretions of Roman Catholicism, Christmas was Christ Mass, a Roman Catholic festival with no biblical reason for existence. Christmas *meant* disloyalty to the biblical revelation, to the pure practice of the Early Church, and to the political independence of Scotland. We must grant that in the sixteenth century Scotch context, Christmas did carry that meaning and ought on biblical grounds to have been banned; but today the context of Christmas has changed. In predominantly Protestant America, there is little likelihood of domination by Rome. Consequently, the biblical grounds which were important to my Scotch ancestors are no longer germane. It does not seem desirable today to ban Christmas. (In passing I might point out the contemporary danger of Christmas becoming merely a commercial carnival; but I shall not have time to develop that thought.) New meanings must be welcomed, changed, or rejected according to their contemporary value plus biblical light.

Inevitably, much room remains for differences of opinion. Is Halloween 'spirit worship' or fun? In Mexico on All Saints Day, a certain kind of bread which Roman Catholics place on the graves of their loved ones is for sale. Can biblical Christians buy and enjoy that bread? When other little children, up and down the block, are enjoying the special bread, should evangelical children also enjoy it or should they abstain? The correct answer depends on the meaning of the bread. If it means feeding the spirits or adhering to Roman Catholic doctrine, Evangelical pastors would no doubt counsel abstaining, but if it means sharing in a pleasant seasonal custom, they would probably counsel identifying with neighbors and eating it.

Christians living under tyranny and gathering to worship in hidden places regard "obedience to the law" according to *that* cultural context. Christians living in a free land where laws are fair and religious liberty is guaranteed read the Bible without fear. They regard "obedience to the law" from a different context. The question "should Christians obey the law" means something very different to each of these groups. Christians living under tyranny gather illegally for worship impelled by conscience itself, quoting the apostolic word that we must obey God rather than men. Christians living under freedom refuse to gather illegally and would quote the Bible to support their refusal.

In short, the meaning of cultural components changes with circumstances, and biblical principals apply to what acts *mean* in specific contexts. Consequently, in all such adjustments, differences of opinion are inevitable. When there is no clear biblical directive, Christians have to do the right as they see the right.

2. Differences arise because some adjustments which will be banned later can be allowed (or cannot be prevented) at the beginning.

Adjustments which are less than ideal are often justified because they are made at the beginning of a Christian movement. They may be all that is possible at an early stage. For instance, take imperfect Sunday observance in the first tiny congregation in some district in Bangladesh. The Fourth Command was given when the Hebrews lived separated from other peoples and could control what happened on the seventh day; but it was also intended to be a pattern for all of God's household everywhere.

In regard to Sunday observance in Bangladesh in 1974, what is pleasing to God? Christians in Bangladesh form only a small fraction of the population and are hired hands working for Moslems. The weekly market is held on Sunday. If Christian women do not market on Sunday they are seriously handicapped, and if Christian men do not work on Sunday they will be fired. Under these circumstances the missionary who is beginning the church decides that weekly worship on Sunday night is justified on bib-

stands the Bible to say. Sunday evening worship is instituted as the best that can be done during the small weak beginnings of the Christian movement in the belief that it is pleasing to God.

As Sunday night worship becomes the custom, Christian leaders might say to themselves, "When this church grows strong and congregations numerous, because we believe the Bible and intend to obey it, we shall institute a full day of rest and worship. The adjustment made now looks forward to better things as soon as they become possible."

Here again, since the variables in each situation are many, good Christians will differ as to whether a given adjustment is biblically justifiable or not. For example, many missions rule that drinking banana beer or rice wine is incompatible with the Christian life and will not baptize drinkers. They argue that unless this curse is stopped at the very beginning, the church will soon be betrayed and debased by drunken Christians and drunken pastors. Much evidence supports the argument. On my last visit to India, members of a congregation told me they vainly begged their pastor to drink only on week days and not to appear in the pulpit while under the influence of liquor. However, since drinking wine is nowhere forbidden in the Bible, and since abstention from it forces the few beginning Christians to sever the normal ties binding them to their relatives and friends, other missions will baptize men who continue to drink banana beer or palm wine.

I use this illustration not to commend either course, but to point out the differences between good Christians as to what beginning adjustments they believe to be *enough in harmony* with biblical precepts to permit them in good conscience.

3. Differences of opinion arise because other "gentiles" must be reached.

As we work toward resolving the clash biblically, we must

remember the extreme importance of *keeping the door open to the unconverted.* Let us look at three examples.

Consider first what adjustment should be made by Christianity in India toward that great cultural component, caste. I take up one specific part of the problem and ask, "Should converts from the upper castes be encouraged to form churches in their neighborhoods made up of upper caste people only?"

In many parts of India, the first castes to turn in considerable numbers to Christianity have been the depressed — the Harijans. The churches therefore are in the sections of the towns and villages where the depressed live. As members of the high castes hear the call of Christ, they find that becoming Christians necessitates being baptized in the church in the Harijan quarter and eating a brotherhood meal with Harijan Christians. Thus to the upper castes, to become a Christian is to become a Harijan. This closes the door to further conversions from the upper castes.

With the picture clearly in mind, the following question may now be posed: Should a *truly Indian Christianity* encourage among upper castes the formation of congregations which, while fully accepting the Bible and all it says about the One Body of Christ, have very little social contact with churches of the depressed classes? Will a *truly Indian Christianity* build churches in the upper caste sections of towns and villages? Some Christians vigorously attack the idea on the basis that biblical Christianity demands instant brotherhood. One who is not willing to worship, eat, and marry across ethnic barriers is not ready to become a Christian! Yet other Christians point out that admirable Christian denominations in Europe and America have very little intercommunion and interdining and no intermarriage with other denominations. In India too, as a matter of fact, many congregations composed largely of people of one ethnic origin never intermarry with Christians of other ethnic backgrounds and have little to do with them. The proposed step turns out to be no innovation, but merely an extension of present practice.

My judgment is that the formation of congregation *in all ethnic units and cultures,* not only in India but in all lands, should be vigorously encouraged. Only this will hold the door open to the unconverted. The degree to which each church in its daily life *achieves* full brotherhood with churches of differing educational, economic and ethnic character is important, but must not be the one criterion on which the expansion of the Faith hinges.

In the Philippines, cock fighting has been universally banned by Protestant Christians. It is accompanied by gambling and poverty. The principal of a Christian school in Leyte told me that when he became a Christian he sold his seventeen fighting cocks and experienced a marked financial improvement. His new style of life also cut him off from his old companions and to a degree closed the door to further conversion from the cock fighting fraternity. Although cock fighting is not prohibited in the Bible, my present judgment is that the Protestant Church does well to discourage this colorful component of Philippine culture. The door to the unconverted must be kept open as much as possible, but the economic potential of the Christian community must also be enhanced.

The hottest topic in Christian circles in Africa for many years has been polygamy, practiced by the stronger, richer men of most tribes. Polygamy is nowhere prohibited in the Bible; indeed, the Old Testament tells of many men approved by God having several wives. Yet polygamy as a system is only tolerated in the Old Testament. It is not endorsed, much less commended. Polygamy unquestionably is a social evil and is judged so by African leaders and educated African women. It might be rationally defended as just when large numbers of men have been killed off in war; but when numbers of men and women are equal, polygamy by definition means that many men are left without wives — an obviously unjust state of affairs. All this brings us to the question: Shall we baptize believers who, while still non-Christians, had legally married several wives? If only such as renounce all wives but one can be baptized, then each man baptized closes the door to other polygamists. The situation will be entirely otherwise when, by the year 2025, let us say, the main African populations south of the Sahara will have grown up in the Church and will therefore marry within an established system of monogamy.

The exact question regarding this component of culture is this: Since there is no biblical prohibition against baptizing men who, as non-Christians in accord with their religion and culture, have married more than one wife, and since it is of importance to keep conversion a real option to the stronger, wealthier men who comprise the power structure of each village, should the Church, without relaxing its rules against *Christians* taking second wives, allow the baptism of polygamists coming in from non-Christian religions?

What the last three examples have been exploring is whether in some cultural components *an interim adjustment* may be allowed. I have suggested that in the case of the third command under the circumstances described, the answer should be yes. In the case of cock fighting, the answer should be no. And in the case of baptizing penitent polygamist believers from non-Christian faiths, the answer should be yes. Disagreement in each case among Christians simply underlines the fact that the farther away each instance gets from clear biblical directives, the greater the room for honest differences of opinion.

4. Differences of opinion arise because most adjustments are of secondary importance only and men feel free to differ about them.

Of primary importance are the factors which build up the spiritual health of the emerging church — intensive study of the Bible, powerful preaching of the Gospel, fervent prayer, conscious obedience to the living Lord, practice of Christian principles, revival, and dedication. Where these mark emerging churches, adjustments and accommodations are of minor importance. One missiologist will say that an adjustment which ought to have been made was not made. Another believes that an accommodation to the culture was allowed mistakenly. A third may hold that an erroneous doctrine was taught for a season. But all agree that these errors are not fatal if spiritual health is high. They will be righted if the Bible is believed and taught as the infallible, inspired Word of God. The Holy Spirit will overrule and guide dedicated Christians into all truth.

Cordially affirming this, it is nevertheless true that spiritual health *plus informed appreciation of adjustments to cultures and their component parts* is a desirable goal, particularly where the Church is advancing on new ground. As Christianity One spreads from culture to culture, it must not be unnecessarily burdened or stopped by inflicting on weak churches adjustments and patterns which suited strong churches in other cultures. The church should not apply the biblical principles of Christianity One without knowing and taking into account the cultural context.

EPILOGUE

The prophet Isaiah looks forward to a time when men of many different cultures will beat their swords into plowshares and their spears into pruning hooks. The steel will still be in the hands of the same men, but since they will obey the Lord, the steel will be put to peaceful uses.

Resolving the clash between One Way and Many Ways does not mean wiping out the Many Ways. After Christianization, most aspects of most cultures — like the steel — will still be there. Irishmen will still glory in wearing the green and Ethiopian rulers will still welcome distinguished visitors with gorgeous tribal dances. The genius of India which built the amazing temples, palaces, and forts of the myriad countries of that wonderful sub-continent will continue to bless the world. The artistry of Japan will grow still more artistic; and so with every culture in every land.

However, the universal revelation of God's will in the Bible and in Jesus Christ will become the common treasure of all cultures. Adherence to it will lead men of every kindred and tongue to beat all their "swords" — damaging cultural components — into "plowshares," and all their "spears" — harmful customs — into "pruning hooks." The riches of all cultures will flow into the Holy City.

Blake sang: I shall not cease from mental strife,
              Nor shall the sword sleep in my hand,
              Till we have built Jerusalem,
              In England's green and pleasant land.

That is the goal toward which we journey — building Jerusa-
lems in all green and pleasant lands. Each Holy City will be
enriched by its own culture. All its cultural components will be
purified by the written Word. Each People of God will be filled
with the Holy Spirit. Each city will be different from all others,
and yet each will be Jerusalem. All of its citizens will walk in
the Light.

The vision of St. John in The Revelation is of great significance here. In that city, he writes, the "leaves of the tree were
for the healing of *ta ethne.*" The *ethne*, the peoples, the languages will all be there. But in the cultures which enter that city
"there shall no more be anything accursed [no more swords,
no more spears, no more cultural components which are displeas-
ing to God], but the throne of God and of the Lamb shall be
in it, and his servants shall worship him; they shall see his face,
and his name shall be on their foreheads. And . . . the Lord God
will be their light" (Rev. 22:2 ff.).

NOTES

CHAPTER 1

1. Blaise Levai, *Ask an Indian About India* (New York: Friendship Press, 1972), pp. 84-85.
2. Richard Niebuhr, *Christ and Culture* (New York: Harper & Bros., 1951), pp. 10-11.
3. Ibid., p. 29.
4. Ibid., p. 28.
5. Ibid., p. 190.

CHAPTER 2

1. Arlene S. Skolnick and Jerome H. Skolnick, *The Family In Transition: Rethinking Marriage, Sexuality, Child Rearing, and Family Organization* (Boston: Little, Brown, 1971), p. 463 f.
2. Kenneth S. Latourette, *The Thousand Years of Uncertainty,* vol. 2 in *A History of the Expansion of Christianity* (New York: Harper & Bros., 1938), pp. 413-414.
3. L. J. Latham, *Teaching Bible to Thai Youth* (an unpublished thesis in the School of Theology, Fuller Theological Seminary, Pasadena, California), pp. 78-79.
4. Os Guinness, "The East, No Exit," *Eternity,* December 1973, p. 26.

CHAPTER 3

1. Walter Goldschmidt, *Comparative Functionalism: An Essay in Anthropological Theory* (Berkeley: University of California Press, 1966), p. 134.
2. Lloyd Kwast, *Crucial Issues in Missions Tomorrow,* ed. by Donald McGavran (Chicago: Moody Press, 1972), p. 166.
3. In *The Bulletin of the Society for African Church History,* vol. 3, nos. 1-2, p. 24, edited by A. F. Walls, University of Aberdeen.

CHAPTER 4

1. Geoffrey Bromiley, *Eternity,* August 1970, p. 12.
2. G. C. Oosthuizen, *Theological Battleground in Asia and Africa* (New York: Humanities Press, Inc., 1972), pp. 23-24.
3. M. M. Thomas, *The Acknowledged Christ of the Indian Renaissance* (Naperville [Ill.]: Allenson, 1969), p.315.
4. Oosthuizen, p. 28.
5. Ibid., p. 25.
6. Ibid.
7. George Forell, *The Proclamation of the Gospel in a Pluralistic World* (Philadelphia: Fortress Press, 1973), p. 64.
8. Bromiley, *Eternity,* p. 12.